INTERNATIO
SOCIALISI

A quarterly journal of socialist theory

Autumn 1999
Contents

Issue 84 of INTERNATIONAL SOCIALISM, quarterly journal of the Socialist Workers Party (Britain)

Published September 1999
Copyright © International Socialism
Distribution/subscriptions: International Socialism,
PO Box 82, London E3
American distribution: B de Boer, 113 East Center Street, Nutley,
New Jersey 07110
Subscriptions and back copies: PO Box 16085, Chicago
Illinois 60616
Editorial and production: 0207 538 5821
Sales and subscriptions: 0207 531 9810
American sales: 773 665 7337

ISBN 1 898876 59 3

Printed by BPC Wheatons Ltd, Exeter, England
Typeset by East End Offset, London E3
Cover by Sherborne Design Ltd

For details of back copies see the end pages of this book

Subscription rates for one year (four issues) are:

Britain and overseas (surface):	individual	£14 ($30)
	institutional	£25
Air speeded supplement:	North America	£3
	Europe/South America	£3
	elsewhere	£4

Note to contributors
The deadline for articles intended for issue 86 of
International Socialism is 1 December 1999

All contributions should be double spaced with wide margins.
Please submit two copies. If you write your contribution
using a computer, please also supply a disk, together with
details of the computer and program used.

INTERNATIONAL
SOCIALISM ★

A quarterly journal of socialist theory

FROM DAGESTAN to Scotland, from the Balkans to Indonesia, the language of ethnic conflict has become the common coin of political debate, seemingly replacing earlier concepts like oppression and racism. Neil Davidson argues that looking at the world through the glass of ethnic division obscures real issues of oppression, disguising the ways in which ethnic characteristics are foisted on local populations by the Great Powers. Even when, as a result of oppression or social dislocation, such populations come to adopt the ethnic identity as their own, such definitions should not be uncritically accepted by the left since they obscure class divisions and power relations.

REFUGEES COMING to Europe have quickly found that the politics of ethnic characterisation can be little more than a cover for refurbished imperial racism, as Phil Marfleet shows in his study of the emerging ideology of the European Union's policy of 'Fortress Europe'. But Europe also has another face. Jim Wolfreys shows in impressive detail that the class struggles in France since the great public sector strikes of 1995 have transformed the political landscape, wounding the right and opening new opportunities for the left. Mike Gonzalez's interview with Tom Behan looks at Rifondazione, the reborn Italian Communist Party's attempt to fill the vacuum on the left.

THE INTERNATIONAL BRIGADES are one of the most famous examples of internationalism in working class history. Andy Durgan, historical adviser on Ken Loach's *Land and Freedom,* assesses their impact in the Spanish Civil War. John Molyneux replies to criticism of his assessment of modern art and Judy Cox welcomes Brian Manning's *The Far Left in the English Revolution.*

The trouble with 'ethnicity'

NEIL DAVIDSON

The concept of exploitation is central to the Marxist understanding of history and contemporary society. But not all social conflicts can be immediately reduced to the struggle between exploiters and exploited, and to explain these conflicts we require other concepts. The most important is that of oppression. This refers to systematic discrimination by one social group against another on the grounds of characteristics either inherited (skin colour, gender) or socially acquired (religious belief, sexual orientation). The experience of oppression cuts across class lines, although that experience is more or less severe depending on where its victims are placed within the class structure. Some forms, like the oppression of women, have persisted throughout the existence of class society, while others, like racism, are specific to capitalism alone. Sometimes the reasons, or pretexts, for the oppression of a group may change over time. During the feudal era, for example, Jewish people were persecuted for their religious beliefs, but as capitalism developed persecution increasingly took place on the grounds of their supposed race. Whatever the reason or pretext, however, ruling classes throughout history have instigated or endorsed the oppression of different groups in order to maintain or create divisions amongst those over whom they rule. Recently, groups have increasingly been subjected to oppression on the grounds of their ethnicity. The most extreme form of such oppression has become known as 'ethnic cleansing'.

The term 'ethnic cleansing' is an English translation of the Serbo-Croat phrase *etnicko ciscenje*. It was first used in Yugoslavia, not in the conflicts which erupted after the end of the Cold War, but by the Croatian Ustashe during the Second World War to describe its policy of killing or expelling Serbs, Jews, Gypsies and Muslims from the fascist state the Ustashe briefly set up with Nazi support. The first use during the current events was by the Croatian Supreme Council in 1991, after the Croatian declaration of independence from Yugoslavia, to describe the actions of Serb guerrillas who were attempting to drive Croats out of areas where Serbs were in the majority: 'The aim of this expulsion is obviously the 'ethnic cleansing' of the critical areas [to] be annexed to Serbia.' The phrase only began to appear in the British press—and thereafter in popular usage—during the war which began in Bosnia-Hercegovina the following year, when Bosnian Serb forces, initially backed by the Milosevic regime in Belgrade, started expelling Muslims and Croats from those parts of the state territory that the Bosnian Serbs considered to be Serbian.[1]

Since then the term has been used not just to describe events in former Yugoslavia (where all sides became involved in the practice to some extent), but in similar—and in some cases even worse—occurrences distant in space and time. On the one hand, the term was being extended *spatially* to events, such as the massacres in Rwanda during 1994, which took place in societies geographically distant from Yugoslavia and were quite different in terms of their historical development. On the other hand, the term was also extended *chronologically* back to events, such as the expulsion and killing of Armenians by Turks at the end of the First World War, that were historically distant and had not previously been discussed in these terms.[2]

'Ethnic cleansing' presupposes the existence of different ethnic groups. The majority of people who opposed the bombing of Yugoslavia also opposed the 'ethnic cleansing' of Kosovan Albanians which NATO used to justify it, arguing that it both intensified the hatreds which made ethnic cleansing possible and made it easier to carry out by forcing the removal of the international monitors who had provided some check on the Serb paramilitaries. However, the opponents of the war tended to share with supporters of the war—and indeed with the people carrying out the 'ethnic cleansing'—the view that there were genuine ethnic differences between groups in former Yugoslavia. From the anti-war perspective, ethnic differences such as those between the Serbs and the Kosovan Albanians should be mutually respected rather than made the occasion for oppression, but the differences themselves could and should not be denied. This position is inadequate, and I want to argue instead that we need to go beyond opposition to 'ethnic cleansing'—which of course means all 'ethnic cleansing', not only that of the Kosovan Albanians—and question the validity of the term ethnicity itself.

Since the argument that follows may be liable to misrepresentation, I should perhaps make one central point clear from the start. Ethnicity is often equated with culture, most frequently with that of minority populations in Western Europe and North America, or with non-Western cultures more generally. Older readers may remember a time in the late 1960s and early 1970s when Guatemalan pottery or Afghan textiles were regularly described as 'ethnic' when being marketed in Britain, as if 'ethnicity' was some special property which they possessed. I am not arguing against cultural diversity, still less suggesting that socialists should abandon their duty to defend people whose culture is under threat, or who are suffering from any of the other forms of oppression outlined above. Nearly 100 years ago, Lenin pointed out the necessity for socialists to be 'tribunes of the people' in words which still retain their relevance: 'Working class consciousness cannot be genuine political consciousness unless the workers are trained to respond to all cases of tyranny, oppression, violence and abuse, no matter what class is affected—unless they are trained, moreover, to respond from a social democratic [ie revolutionary socialist] point of view and no other'.[3] For socialists, therefore, it makes no difference whether particular groups of people are oppressed because of their language, religion, nationhood, or ethnicity. In each case our duty is to defend the oppressed and show solidarity with them, particularly where socialists themselves belong to the dominant linguistic, religious, national or—assuming for the moment that such a thing exists—ethnic group.

My point is rather that the way in which the notion of 'ethnicity' is currently and increasingly being used contains a number of problems for the left. Two stand out in particular. On the on hand, those who approve of ethnicity as the affirmation of a cultural identity, in so far as they emphasise supposedly innate differences between human social groups, are in danger of opening the door to the current form of racist ideology. On the other hand, those who disapprove of ethnicity as a manifestation of (real or imagined) exclusionist tribalism are in danger, in so far as they suggest that 'ethnic' nationalisms are particularly prone to oppressive behaviour, of obscuring those characteristics which all nationalisms have in common, whether they are oppressor, oppressed, or fall into neither of these categories. Our first task is therefore to distinguish between the various ways in which the term 'ethnicity' has been used, and assess their respective validity.

Kinship, occupation and identity

'Ethnicity' has been defined in three ways: first, where members of a group have a common line of descent, and consequently a shared *kinship*; second, where they have a common position within the international division of labour and consequently a shared *occupation*; third, where they have one or more cultural attributes in common and consequently a shared *identity*. The first and second reasons assume that ethnicity can be defined objectively, the third that it can be defined subjectively. As we shall see, it is this subjective definition which is currently dominant.

Kinship: Social groups which share a common line of descent are usually referred to in anthropology as endogamous groups, or groups whose members interbreed exclusively with each other, thus maintaining the same genetic inheritance. Such groups would have been universal at the origins of human evolution but are, however, virtually impossible to find today. Indeed, recent archaeological and anthropological work suggests that mass human migration—often across entire continents —occurred much earlier in history than was previously believed, and resulted in the erosion of endogamy within the original tribal societies. One writer notes that as a result of these factors, within tribal society 'the common ancestry of "the people" was always partially fictive'.[4] But once we move onto the terrain of recorded history the multiple genetic inheritance of the global population is an indisputable fact that also makes the existence of different 'races' impossible to sustain. Susan Reynolds has rightly criticised the tendency among medieval historians to describe the barbarian invaders of the Roman Empire as biologically distinct 'tribal' entities, simply because of the continued use of their original group name. 'This must be wrong,' she points out. 'Once barbarians had been converted to orthodox Christianity and prohibitions on intermarriage had been lifted, it must have been hard to distinguish them from "Romans" who were already mixed genetically and were increasingly barbarised culturally'.[5]

The main constituent nations of Britain are a case in point. Early in the 18th century Daniel Defoe mocked the pretensions of his countrymen to ethnic purity in his satirical poem, 'The True-Born Englishman':

> *In eager rapes, and furious lust begot,*
> *Between a painted **Briton** and a **Scot**:*
> *Whose gen'ring offspring quickly learnt to bow.*
> *And yoke their heifers to the **Roman** plough:*
> *From whence a mongrel half-bred race there came,*
> *With neither name nor nation, speech or fame:*
> *In whose hot veins now mixtures quickly ran,*
> *Infus'd betwixt a **Saxon** and a **Dane**.*
> *While their rank daughters, to their parents just,*
> *Receiv'd all nations with promiscuous lust.*
> *This nauseous brood directly did contain,*
> *The well-extracted blood of Englishmen.*

As Linda Colley comments, 'Defoe's uncompromising insistence on the ethnic diversity of England, its early exposure to successive invasions from continental Europe, and the constant intermingling of its people with the Welsh and Scots, was fully justified in historical terms'.[6] Similar intermingling took place in Scotland during the 'Dark Ages' between 400 and 1057. 'The period has, with justice, been called "an age of migrations",' writes Michael Lynch, 'when the different tribal peoples—Picts, Scots, Angles, Britons and Scandinavians—who inhabited the mainland of modern day Scotland moved, fought, displaced and intermarried with each other'.[7] And to these, of course, could be added the Norman English who were invited to settle in Scotland during the reign of David I (1124-1153), and who were themselves descended from Viking settlers in part of what is now France.

In an extreme case like that of the native Australians it might be supposed that endogamy was maintained until the arrival of the European colonists, but in fact they too had interbred with Papuan and Polynesian immigrants many centuries before the Dutch or the British set foot on their continent.[8] As the late Eric Wolf wrote of the ethnic composition of the world in 1400, 'If there were any isolated societies these were but temporary phenomena—a group pushed to the edge of a zone of interaction and left to itself for a brief moment in time'.[9] In short, even *before* capitalism had penetrated all corners of the world in the search for markets and raw materials, the growth of trade, conquest and migration had already made the existence of endogamous gene pools increasingly rare. Of course, this does not mean that various groups have not claimed, and in some cases perhaps even believed, that they were descended from the pure stock of some ancestral group, but it is important to understand that these claims and beliefs are based on a myth of kinship, not a reality.

Occupation: Like the modern notion of 'race', the origins of this second definition lie in the colonial expansion of capitalism outside of its European heartlands. From the origins of systemic racial slavery in the 16th century, 'race' has been a general term to override differences between different peoples by categorising them on the basis of physical characteristics, of which skin colour was the most important—although, as we shall see below, the instances of racism directed against the Catholic Irish and by extension the Highland Scots were exceptions in that they were based on religion and language rather than physical appearance.[10] There were massive differences in terms of social development between the Shona speaking peoples of southern Africa who built and lived in the stone city of Great Zimbabwe during the 15th and 16th centuries and the hunter-gatherers who inhabited Australia at the same time. Yet to ideologists of 'race' they were both indistinguishably 'black'. At first racism was used to justify the allocation of specific roles within the system during the process of primitive accumulation (ie as slaves), but latterly racism was used to consign members of 'races' who had migrated to the metropolitan centres to become either part of the reserve army of labour or workers with the worst pay and conditions in the labour force.

'Ethnicity', on the other hand, was a term designed to distinguish between groups within overall 'racial' categories in those sections of the labour market in which they had established themselves. The capitalist mode of production requires the subordination of labour to capital, but in the European colonies it also required that the labour force was internally divided. As Eric Wolf notes, the allocation of workers to invented ethnic categories is doubly effective in this respect, first 'by ordering the groups and categories of labourers hierarchically with respect to one another', and second 'by continuously producing and recreating symbolically marked "cultural" distinctions among them'. On the one hand, groups were allocated specific roles both within the production process and within social life more generally. On the other hand, they were encouraged to identify with these roles and to defend them against other groups. Wolf is therefore right to say that these ethnic identities are not ' "primordial" social relationships', but 'historical products of labour market segmentation under the capitalist mode [of production]'.[11] Sometimes these built on existing division of labour within pre-colonial society; sometimes they were wholly new and based on the division of labour within the new industries that the colonists established.

In Rwanda and Burundi before colonisation there were three distinct groups—the Twas, the Hutus and the Tutsis. The most numerically significant were the Hutus and the Tutsis, membership of which passed down through the male side of the family.[12] Is this an example of 'kinship' ethnicity which I earlier consigned to prehistory? In fact, although group membership at birth was based on that of the male parent, it was possible to move from the Tutsis to the Hutus in the course of life. All three groups spoke the same language, and the distinctions between them were principally based on the fact that they performed different social roles: the Hutu in farming, the Tutsi in cattle rearing and the Twa in hunting. A cattle owner was a Tutsi by definition, which meant that Hutus could 'become' Tutsis if they were able to accumulate sufficient wealth to become cattle owners themselves, a transition that was marked ceremonially. Since longhorn cattle were the main form of disposable property, people who owned cattle were therefore a significant part of the ruling class, but there were also Tutsis who owned few cattle and whose social position was proportionally less important.

The situation is further complicated by the fact that Hutus were members of that section of the ruling class who owned large farms, without becoming Tutsis. As Charlie Kimber writes, 'The Hutu-Tutsi distinction in pre-colonial

Rwanda and Burundi was not a simple class distinction (because you could be a poor Tutsi or a rich Hutu), nor was it an ethnic distinction (because you could be born into one group and die as another)'.[13] It did, however, become an ethnic distinction with the arrival first of the German and then the Belgian colonial administrations. Under these regimes, real occupational stratification which designated people as being Hutu, Tutsi and Twa was transformed into imaginary ethnic distinctions between separate 'tribal' groups, one of whom (the Tutsis) was privileged over the others in the colonial hierarchy and in the immediately post-colonial state.

Rwanda shows how the existing occupational roles of existing populations can become the basis of new ethnicities imposed by colonialism. More commonly, ethnicities have developed among migrant groups responding to dislocation and industrialisation, as the emergence of ethnicity in the Gezira region of the Sudan after the beginning of cotton production in 1925 demonstrates. Some of the workers recruited by the British migrated for this purpose from various West African groups, all of whom were Muslims and most of whom spoke Hausa. Unlike the local Sudanese, these immigrants were already accustomed to wage labour in their own homelands, which had been industrialised earlier, and were consequently more likely to meet their quotas. The British tended to replace local workers with the immigrants. In response to their displacement, the Sudanese began to refer disparagingly to the West Africans as 'Fellata', a term which has overtones of slavish obedience. The West Africans in turn began to distinguish themselves from the Sudanese precisely on the basis of their supposedly greater capacity for hard work, a distinction linked to the adoption of a fundamentalist Islam far stricter than that practised by the Sudanese, and which was enshrined in their self description as 'Takari', a respectful term to describe pilgrims to Mecca from West Africa. As Eriksen concludes from this episode, 'Contemporary ethnicity or "tribalism" is not, in other words, a relic of the past but a product of modernisation processes leading up to the present'.[14]

The sugar industry in the French colony of Mauritius provides an extreme example of how a wide range of characteristics can be fitted to occupational roles, becoming ethnicities as a result. Indians—members of a national group—were recruited as labourers in the canefields. Brahmins from among these Indians—adherents of a religious sect— were made foremen. Creoles—descendants of slaves and consequently identifiable by their skin colour—tended to be skilled workers. Chinese or 'Mulattos' ('half-castes')—a national group and one defined by skin colour—held the middle managerial positions. The estate managers were invariably French settlers, who were both a national group and identifiable by their white skin but, needless to say, they were not considered to have an 'ethnicity'.[15]

We might say, therefore, that the term 'ethnicity' is valid in this sense where it is used to describe the way in which existing occupational patterns in pre-capitalist societies were used by European colonists to classify the population as supposedly endogamous groups, or where the migrations set in train by colonialism had led groups to define themselves as either endogamous, or in possession of some quality or characteristic which distinguished them from the native populations around them. What has confused the issue is that the word 'ethnicity' was not in general use at the time these developments were taking place (roughly between 1875 and 1945), but this would not be the first time that something has existed in the world before the language has been developed to describe it.[16] Nevertheless, it could be usefully employed now in relation, for example, to the situation of Chinese traders in Indonesia or Korean traders in Los Angeles. But the term is generally not used with this degree of specificity. On the contrary, it is the third and final notion of 'ethnicity'—that of identity—which is currently sweeping all before it.

Identity: In answer to the central question of why groups come to identify themselves as having a particular 'ethnicity', Anthony Smith has argued that an ethnic community—that is, a community whose members have not had their 'ethnicity' imposed on them from outside, but distinguish themselves in this way—has six main attributes: 'a collective proper name, a myth of common ancestry, shared historical memories, one or more differentiating elements of common culture, an association with a specific "homeland", and a sense of solidarity for significant sectors of the population'.[17] This attempts to incorporate a belief in kinship relations as part of the definition. It is not clear why these are 'ethnic' attributes rather than simply 'national' ones. Indeed, the definition of a nation given a few pages earlier by Smith could be substituted without affecting his argument: 'A nation can therefore be defined as a named human population sharing an historic territory, common myths and historical territories, a mass public culture, a common economy, and common legal rights and duties for all members'.[18] (The similarity is perhaps unsurprising, given that Smith is attempting to argue for the importance of ethnicity in the formation of national identity.) It is perfectly possible for a particular social group to identify themselves as having an 'ethnic' identity without possessing all or any of the attributes listed by Smith, as the example of the Bosnian Muslims makes clear. Like all classificatory lists, the elements are completely arbitrary. Perhaps in realisation of this, some writers have abandoned any attempts at precise definition.

In 1953 David Reisman became the first person to use the term 'ethnicity' to mean identity and he was quickly followed in this by other North American sociologists.[19] In their hands the term was used to describe those groups who did not belong to the white Anglo-Saxon Protestant (WASP) population—that is to say, everyone who was not descended from the original English, Scottish, and 'Scots' Irish (Protestant Irish) settlers. Exceptionally, German immigrants were allowed to merge with the WASPs, at least where they too were Protestants.[20] Ethnicity was therefore reserved for 'minorities' identified by attributes as diverse as skin colour (blacks), religion (Jews) or country of origin (Italians). This lack of specificity brings to mind the famous conversation between Humpty Dumpty and Alice during her adventures through the looking glass:

> *'When I use a word,' Humpty Dumpty said, in a rather scornful tone, 'it means just what I choose it to mean—neither more nor less.' 'The question is,' said Alice, 'whether you can make words mean so many different things.' 'The question is,' said Humpty Dumpty, 'which is to be the master—that's all'.*[21]

Stuart Hall, here playing the role of Humpty Dumpty, has offered the following definition of 'ethnicity': 'By "ethnicity" we mean the commitment to those points of attachment which give the individual some sense of "place" and position in the world, whether these be in relation to particular communities, localities, territories, languages, religions or cultures'.[22] If the term encompasses 'communities, localities, territories, languages, religions or cultures', then it is difficult to see what could not be defined as 'ethnic'. A US sociologist, Abner Cohen, once proposed that City of London stockbrokers should be considered an 'ethnic' group by virtue of their group identity.[23] He was not being entirely serious, but the proposal takes the logic of 'ethnic identity' to its conclusion in Bedlam. More seriously, the census which British citizens will be required to complete in 2001 asks respondents to define their own 'ethnicity' from a core list which consists of four nations (Bangladesh, China, India and Pakistan), one continent (Asia) and two skin colours (black and white)—although these are subdivided, the first into 'Black: African', 'Black: Caribbean' and 'Black: Other', and the latter into 'White: British' and 'White: Other'. In fact, most uses of the word 'ethnic' are in place of some other word (like 'communities, localities, territories, languages, religions or cultures'), the use of which would give far greater precision of meaning. The result of not doing so, as the South African Marxist Neville Alexander rightly says, is 'to reduce the diverse reasons for the emergence of group solidarities to a single quality called "ethnicity", thereby obscuring precisely what has to be explained—the basis of such solidarity'.[24] Ethnicity, in short, becomes a way of labelling people through the use of an ideological super-category that includes virtually any characteristic they might conceivably possess.

There is a further problem. Hall assumes that 'ethnicity' can be divided into 'bad' and 'good' forms that more or less correspond to that of the majority populations of metropolitan imperialist states on the one hand and of their minority immigrant communities on the other. Of the former, Hall writes, 'In the face of the proliferation of cultural differences, and the multi-ethnic character of the new Britain, and threatened on the other side by the encroaching trauma of an emerging European identity, we have seen over the past decade a particularly defensive, closed and exclusive definition of "Englishness" being advanced as a way of warding off or refusing to live with difference—a retreat from modernity no exercise in managerial newspeak or the "new entrepreneurialism" can disguise or deflect'.[25] Of the latter, however, we learn that it is 'not an ethnicity which is doomed to survive, as Englishness was, only by marginalising, dispossessing, displacing and forgetting other ethnicities'. On the contrary, these immigrant communities have a 'politics of ethnicity predicated on difference and diversity'.[26] It is difficult to see how Hall could explain conflict between youth of Afro-Caribbean and south Asian descent on this basis (or indeed, that between those of Afro-Caribbean and Korean descent in Los Angeles). And while a model of 'ethnicity' derived from the British (or rather 'English') experience can certainly be generalised to other Western European imperialist nations like France, in a region like the Balkans, where historically there has never been a dominant 'ethnic' group, it has no explanatory power whatsoever.

The internationalisation of capital, crisis and identity politics

The editors of a recent reader on ethnicity begin by reflecting on the sudden upsurge of interest in their subject:

> *For at least 150 years liberals and socialists confidently expected the demise of ethnic, racial and national ties and the unification of the world through international trade and mass communications. These expectations have not been realised. Instead we are witnessing a series of explosive ethnic revivals across the globe. In Europe and the Americas ethnic movements unexpectedly surfaced from the 1960s and 1970s, in Africa and Asia they have been gaining force since the 1950s, and the demise of the former Soviet Union has encouraged ethnic conflicts and national movements to flourish throughout its territory. Since 1990, 20 new states based largely upon dominant ethnic communities have been recognised. Clearly ethnicity, far from fading away, has now become a central issue in the social and political life of every continent. The 'end of history', it seems, turns out to have ushered in the era of ethnicity.*[27]

Why has the upsurge of 'ethnic' identification taken place now? For this sense of 'ethnicity' to become established required two general conditions. The first condition is the need to distinguish one group from another. As Thomas Eriksen has stressed, 'Ethnicity is essentially an aspect of a relationship, not a property of a group.' In other words, cultural distinctiveness in itself does not confer 'ethnicity' on a group, but only when it is contrasted with the culture of another group: 'For ethnicity to come about, the groups must have a minimum of contact with each other, and they must entertain ideas of each other as being culturally different from themselves'.[28] But for this to happen the differences must themselves be considered important, and there are only certain circumstances in which this is the case. The most important of these circumstances, and the second condition, is rapid social change. As Malcolm Cross notes, 'A man living in a world where change is largely absent does not need to be reminded of his culture in order to affirm his identity'.[29] Where that change is destructive of established ways of life— and in some cases whole societies—and class politics does not offer an alternative, then distinguishing oneself as part of a specific group in order to struggle over the resources, or scavenge what you can from the rubble left by the onward march of international capital, may appear to be the only available option even where group membership may previously have meant little or nothing to the people concerned.

Across the developing world in particular, the state is increasingly failing to deliver any form of social redistribution to the most disadvantaged. And some areas, most of which are in Africa, have seen not just increasing poverty but actual social collapse, brought on by economic crisis, which the state has been unable to prevent. In these circumstances an 'ethnic' community, often constructed by colonial powers that have long since departed, can provide what the state cannot. As David Brown notes, 'If the state claiming to be the cultural nation cannot offer the necessary protection, then it is the cultural nation claiming to be the potential state which offers the next best bet'.[30] Rwanda provides a particularly tragic example of what can result from the residue of Western invented 'ethnicities' in a situation of acute social crisis. The genocide of 1994, far from being the expression of age old 'ethnic' animosities, was prepared by the destructive impact of colonialism on Central Africa.

The left should be at the forefront of opposition to this, reasserting the realities of class against the myths of ethnicity, but all too often it is handicapped by its refusal to accept that 'identity' can ever be irrelevant, or mystified, or simply a cover for sectional interests. As Adam Kuper writes, 'So although the popular American notion of cultural identity has been stretched beyond ethnic groups to other kinds of minorities, it remains doubly essentialist: one has an essential identity, and this derives from the essential characteristic of the collectivity to which one belongs'.[31] In most cases, however, there are no 'essential' characteristics—nor, indeed, have many of these collectivities existed for any length of time: 'In actuality, a sense of ethnic community can develop among individuals who neither share significant cultural attributes nor who are particularly distinctive from their neighbours; and it can refer to commonalties of circumstance which developed within living memory, and to attributes which clearly do not objectively derive from common ancestry'.[32] The more developed world—in this case the Balkans—provides us with the best example of how, unlike Central Africa, 'ethnicities' can arise with virtually no prior basis.

Unlike their parents, or even their grandparents, many of the people who came to be described as 'ethnic Muslims' in Bosnia-Hercegovina had never been inside a mosque in their lives—at least until they began to be identified in this way for the purposes of persecution, when religion took on a new significance for them. As this example suggests, the distinction between 'imposed' and 'chosen' ethnic identities is not one which can be sustained, since there are many cases where groups which have been identified as possessing a particular attribute and discriminated against on that basis have subsequently chosen to militantly assert that identity in response to their oppressors. But this process is not inevitable. As Misha Glenny writes of the Bosnian Muslims, 'Although largely secular, the explicit religious origins of the Muslims' identity (they have no specific ethnic or linguistic criteria to differentiate themselves from Serbs or Croats, neither do they have a Belgrade or Zagreb to turn to for material, political or spiritual aid) have made the process of defining their nationhood exceptionally difficult.' It is interesting that Glenny, who is otherwise one of the most insightful commentators on the Balkan situation, sees this as a problem, rather than a hopeful basis for overcoming the divisions within Bosnian society, noting that 'many Muslims incline towards aspects of either Serbian or Croatian culture'.[33] But before sides became fixed in the Bosnian war it was by no means certain that residual religious belief would be inflated until it became an imaginary essence by which people were defined: 'Before the war...when the Serbs still hoped to keep Bosnia in Yugoslavia, the media frequently highlighted similarities with the Muslims, while Croats often stressed that Bosnia had been part of historical Croatia and that most Bosnian Muslims were originally of Croatian descent'.[34] In other words, these Muslims could have been absorbed into either Serb or Croat 'ethnicities', in which case the supposedly essential nature of their Islamic identity would never have arisen.

The developed world has not remained untouched by the rise of—or perhaps one should say the retreat to—'ethnicity'. The crisis in Western Europe and North America is clearly not of the same order as that in the Balkans, still less Central Africa, but similar pressures are at work. Where reforms are increasingly hard to come by, two collective solutions remain for improving conditions. One is the road of class struggle, of forcing redistribution either directly from the bourgeoisie in the form of higher wages and better conditions, or indirectly by forcing the state to intervene through legislation or increased taxation. The other road, the road more frequently travelled, is not to struggle for redistribution from the capitalist class to the working class, but to struggle—or more precisely, to lobby—for resources to be redistributed from one section of the working class to another, or from one region to another, or from one 'ethnic' group to another. If groups can become politically organised, and consequently put electoral pressure on local or national politicians, they, or more usually their representatives, can campaign for 'affirmative action' on their behalf.[35]

The latter strategy has a long history in post-war Britain stretching back to the 1960s. It was only after the onset of economic crisis in the 1970s that it came to full maturity. Ambalavaner Sivanandan notes acidly the 'scramble for government favours and government grants…on the basis of specific ethnic needs and problems' by 'minority' groups following the Brixton riots of 1981 and the recommendations of the Scarman Report. The problem is not simply the compromises and downplaying of radical demands which are required to receive state funding, but the fact of competition between communities that increasingly divides them into rival 'ethnic' groups.[36] It is not even the case that such funding as is available invariably goes to the working class areas, since the middle class can play the lobbying game to far greater effect, and will generally reap whatever benefits are to be had.

It would be bad enough if accepting the existence of ethnicity merely meant condoning an endless splintering into rival groups to divide up the crumbs left by global capital, but there are even worse implications. The most serious of these is the relationship between ethnicity and racism.

'Ethnicity' and the new racism

For many on the left (as well as academics and officials in government agencies) it is perfectly acceptable to talk about ethnicity (without quotation marks), whereas it is no longer acceptable to talk about 'race'. There are, in other words, no such things as 'races', but there are such things as 'ethnicities'. As Steve Fenton writes:

> The term race is associated with mistaken science. It connotes physical difference and, frequently, colour. It is typically seen as malign, and racial ideologies have been associated with compulsion and regimes of oppression. By contrast, ethnic can be taken as an analytic term in social science, is often seen as the voluntary identification of peoples, and as (at least potentially) benign.[37]

The problem is that the notion of ethnicity is all too often used to invoke precisely the qualities that used to be invoked under the now discredited notion of 'race'. To understand why, it is necessary to trace the previous major shifts in racist ideology.

Marxist accounts of the origins and development of racist ideology tend to see three moments in the history of capitalism as decisive in determining its precise form. The first is slavery, and the need to justify enslaving millions of fellow human beings at the very moment when men were being declared equal and in possession of certain unalienable rights. The second is colonialism, and the need to justify the conquest and subsequent domination of foreign peoples. The third is immigration, and the need to justify discrimination against peoples who were usually encouraged to come to the metropolitan centres in the process of reconstruction after the Second World War. The respective justifications for the treatment of non-white populations differed in each case, moving from their less than human nature (making it permissible to enslave them) to their backwardness (requiring the guidance of the more advanced white 'races'), to the competition they posed to the white populations for jobs and housing (requiring an end to immigration and in extreme versions the repatriation of existing immigrants).[38] In an important book published in 1981, however, the Marxist philosopher Martin Barker argued that we were now seeing the rise of a 'new racism' which:

> ...can refuse insults: it need never talk of 'niggers', 'wogs' or 'coons'. It does not need to see Jews as morally degenerate, or blacks as 'jungle bunnies'. Nonetheless, in subtle but effective ways it authorises the very emotions of hostility that then get expressed in these terms.[39]

The 'newness' of this racism is not in its reliance on the pseudo-sciences of sociobiology and ethnology for justification—pseudo-science has been a feature of racism from the invention of phrenology in the mid-19th century onwards—but in the claim that it demonstrates the social incompatibility of groups with different cultures. There are two historical precedents for this shift in meaning, in which an entire people were defined by virtue of what had previously been seen as an acquired characteristic—religion in the first, culture more generally in the second—rather than biology.

The first was in Ireland. In his work on the origins of racism, Theodore Allan defines racial oppression as the reduction of 'all members of an oppressed group to an undifferentiated social status, a status beneath that of any member of any social class within the colonising population'. Allan argues that racism originated not from innate propensities on the part of different groups to distinguish themselves from and discriminate against other groups (the 'psycho-cultural' argument), but as a conscious ruling class strategy to justify slavery as an economic system in the epoch where formal male equality was increasingly the norm (the 'socioeconomic' argument). Although his argument is mainly concerned with the racial oppression in the Americas, Allen sees a precursor of white colonial attitudes to the Native Americans and African slaves in the British (ie Lowland Scots and English) treatment of the Irish from the Anglo-Norman period onwards. With the Reformation, however, the religious difference between the Protestantism of the British settlers and the Catholicism of the Irish natives provided an additional element to the prejudices of the former: 'What had fed primarily on simple xenophobia now, as religio-racism, drank at eternal springs of private feelings about "man and god".' There were also more material reasons. As Allan strongly argues, the construction of 'religio-racism' against the entire Irish population was a conscious choice on the part of the English ruling class and its Scottish allies. Ireland was a crucial strategic territory in the struggle between Catholic and Protestant Europe, hence the impossibility of co-opting sections of the Catholic Irish ruling class for the purposes of social control: they could not be trusted to take the British side in the conflicts with Catholic Spain and France. The alternative was to attempt to convert the Catholic population to Protestantism, but this was unthinkable for most of the 18th century for two reasons. First, the Ascendancy comprised a relatively small minority of the population whose wealth and power would have been threatened if a majority had been allowed to share its legal privileges. Second, the majority of Protestants below the ruling class proper were Dissenters, most of them Presbyterians, and consequently excluded from the privileges available to communicants with the Anglican Church of Ireland.

Mass conversion of the Catholic population was likely to lead to the converts joining the Dissenting branch of Protestantism rather than that of the great landowners, raising the prospect of the majority of the population uniting against the Ascendancy. After this came near to happening anyway in 1798, the British ruling class and its Irish extension responded by incorporating the Dissenting element through the Orange Order, but, more importantly, by shifting the nature of Catholic oppression from a racial to a national basis *'by the incorporation of the Irish bourgeoisie into the intermediate buffer social control system'*. In short, once Catholics were allowed to participate in ruling Ireland, the system of 'religio-racial' oppression had to be abandoned.[40] There are problems with this analysis, not least in the explanatory framework where changes are seen as the result of intentional manoeuvres by the ruling class. It is also the case that Irish people in Britain continue to experience racism as the dominant form of oppression. Nevertheless, Allan is clearly right to note that the use of religion—an attribute that we would now regard as 'ethnic'—as the basis of racial identification was rare at the time. In a situation where the oppressed population was the same skin colour as the oppressors, this shift was probably inevitable.

The second precedent was in South Africa. One of the intellectual founders of apartheid (which means 'separate development') in South Africa was W W M Eislen. As Adam Kuper points out, Eislen rejected the notions of black inferiority dominant among his countrymen: 'Not race but culture was the true basis of difference, the sign of destiny.' But, he said, although different cultures should be valued in their own right, their individual integrity should also be preserved: 'If the integrity of traditional cultures were undermined, social disintegration would follow.' Segregation of the races was necessary not to preserve unequal relations between white and black, but the cultural differences between them.[41] This was the theoretical basis on which apartheid was built.

What is disturbing, given these precedents, is that the notion of 'ethnicity', particularly when it is used in its cultural sense, has increasingly become a substitute for 'race', a coded way of reinventing racial categories without making skin colour the key issue, in similar ways to those pioneered in Ireland and South Africa. And it is not simply racists who are responsible for this. The Race Relations Act of 1976 defines a 'racial group...by reference to one or more of the following: colour, race, nationality (including citizenship) or ethnic or national origins'.[42] A Commission for Racial Equality publication setting out the Racial Equality Standard for local government in Scotland asks that 'the Standard should be adopted and used both by authorities that have relatively substantial ethnic minority populations in their areas and those whose ethnic populations are smaller and more scattered'.[43] The assumption that ethnicity represented a minority deviation from a majority norm (is there an 'ethnic majority'?) should in itself make us deeply suspicious, but it is only since the 1970s that the racist undercurrents of the term have become completely obvious. As Neville Alexander points out, quoting one of the US sociologists responsible for popularising the term during the 1940s, 'ethnicity' is useful 'as a means of avoiding the word, yet retaining its meaning'.[44]

Alex Callinicos rightly argues that the 'new' racism has arisen as a result of the discrediting of the notion of biologically distinct races, partly as a result of advances in knowledge which have undermined any scientific basis for such beliefs, and partly (and one suspects far more) as a result of the use to which such beliefs were put during the Holocaust. (Hence the modern convention, which I have followed here, of placing the word 'race' in quotes, indicating that the concept is wholly ideological and has no referent in the world.) Callinicos also argues, however, that the 'newness' of this racism is more apparent than real, since biological racism and, related to this, ideas of black inferiority, are still very much alive and, in any case, the 'new' cultural racism often involves the same type of stereotyping as the 'old' biological racism.[45] There is some force in these criticisms. After reading the attempt by Charles Murray in *The Bell Curve* to explain black underachievement on the basis of genetic inheritance, or an attempt in *The Independent* to distinguish between Serbs and Albanians on the basis of their hair colour, it would be very foolish to predict the disappearance of biological racism. Nevertheless, there are reasons to believe that the dominant form of racist ideology is taking a new form in which questions of 'ethnicity' are central.

First, the emphasis on culture is not related to biology in the sense of indicating that some human beings are genetically superior or inferior to others, but in the sense that human beings are naturally hostile to those with different cultures: '...we may all share a common human nature, but part of that very shared nature is the natural tendency to form bounded social units and to differentiate ourselves from outsiders'.[46] This has become part of the discourse even of the extreme right. During the campaign which preceded the elections to the European Parliament on 10 June 1999, a British National Party leaflet intended for distribution across Scotland called for opposition to the 'uprooting of our culture and to mass immigration', and support for 'the preservation of our unique Scottish identity within a free Britain'. Voters were invited to find out more about the fascist election campaign to save sterling and 'to preserve the cultural and ethnic identity of Scotland and the British people'.[47] The object here is to bait the hook that catches the unwary with references to culture and ethnicity that make a point of *not* referring to racial stereotypes.

Second, and more importantly, we are seeing the naturalisation of 'ethnic' characteristics. Attributes or properties like religion or language that were once regarded as socially acquired and consequently amenable to change *are* increasingly being treated as if they were naturally occurring and permanent. Indeed, in the case of nationalism, Tom Nairn has argued that they are naturally occurring and permanent:

> ...differential cultural development (including language) may have had a function unsuspected by previous historians and theorists... If internal species-diversity through cultural means has always been 'human nature', presumably it will go on being so—in a way that has nothing to do with blood or race.[48]

The idea supported by NATO and large sections of the liberal press—that different 'ethnic' groups in the Balkans 'naturally' want to separate themselves from other groups, if necessary by terror and expulsion—is clearly one practical application of this theory. As long as ethnicity is assumed to have a real existence, then the pressure is always there to accept the logic of these supposed differences—that all the states in the Balkans must have a single dominant 'ethnic' group, no matter what the cost to the other groups who might have lived there for as long or longer.

The same thinking lies behind the Northern Ireland peace agreement. Increasingly the language in which the conflict in the North is described abandons the notions of 'religious sectarianism' in which it was con-ducted for so long, and adopts that of 'ethnic division' instead. Religious belief may decline with secularisation, as it has across most of the British Isles, but if religion has become part of your very nature, then all you can do is keep the two sides ('communities') hermetically sealed from each other. In other words, Protestant and Catholic religious beliefs have become the basis of 'ethnic identities', and these in turn are assumed to function in the same way as 'racial characteristics' once did. In addition to passing over the role that the British state has had in creating and maintaining the conflict, this ideological transformation also has another advantage for the ruling class in that it also absolves it from finding any permanent solution other than 'peaceful coexistence'. The question of language illustrates both how the state pretends to be 'even handed' while supporting the Unionist position, and the way in which the social divisions in the North are treated as 'cultural'.

Since 1968 there has been a revival of interest in Irish culture, and of the Gaelic language in particular, among Catholics in the North. Since this interest has rightly been associated with political Republicanism, or at the very least with the desire to assert a political identity in the face of a state which denies or marginalises it, the educational and cultural activities involved have tended to be organised and financed by the communities themselves rather than by the state. In 1994, however, the government sponsored Cultural Traditions Group expressed its concern that Gaelic was associated with Republicanism and arranged to fund a trust to enable Protestants to learn the language in settings where they would not be trou-bled by these associations. As Bill Rolston points out, this is not 'symmetry' but 'an exercise in depoliticising a cultural movement. It is multiculturalism as counter-insurgency.' The same Cultural Traditions Group also provides funding for the 'Ulster Scots' language, whose sup-porters set up the Ulster Scots society in, by a curious coincidence, 1994.[49] There is no such language (even 'Scottish Scots' is a dialect—in fact several dialects—of English) but such claims help to establish the myth that there are two parallel communities, with equivalent traditions, not a divided society in which one community is oppressed.

The difficulty is that if we lack a word to describe the victims of racism, since we reject the concept of 'race', then the concept of ethnicity seems to offer an alternative. If what I have argued here is correct, however, eth-nicity is rapidly turning into the thing it was originally introduced to oppose. What Adam Kuper has written of contemporary US anthropology seems applicable to much of the left: 'It repudiates the popular ideas that differences are natural, and that cultural identity must be grounded in a primordial, biological identity, but a rhetoric that places great emphasis on difference and identity is not best placed to counter these views. On the contrary, the insistence that radical difference can be observed between peoples best serves to sustain them'.[50]

'Ethnic' versus 'civic' nationalism

There is, however, another danger with the use of 'ethnicity'. It is sometimes argued that 'ethnic' nationalisms that supposedly lead to the purging of entire populations as in Yugoslavia can be combated by an alternative 'civic' nationalism based on politics, not tribe. James Kellas describes this as '"inclusive" in the sense that anyone can adopt that culture and join the nation, even if that person is not considered to be part of the "ethnic nation".'[51] 'Civic' nationalism is frequently presented as the only true form of nationalism. Certain nationalisms—like that of Serbia—are said to be inherently oppressive precisely because they are based on an 'ethnic' identity. The contrast is often made between this kind of nationalism and one described as 'civic' or 'social'—Scottish and Catalan nationalism, for example, are frequently described in this way, not least by Scottish and Catalan nationalists themselves.

George Kerevan, former Trotskyist and currently the SNP spokesperson for the environment, used his column in *The Scotsman* newspaper recently to distinguish the nationalism of his party from that of the Milosevic regime:

> There is nationalism in the sense it applies to Hitler or Milosevic. Call it ethnic or tribal nationalism. In fact, don't call it nationalism at all, because it's not about building modern nations. This is a reactionary, tribal, exclusive ideology espoused in times of economic and political change by those social orders who are being usurped or threatened by the process of modernisation... But there is another, totally different meaning of the word nationalism—nation building. Building the common institutions of an inclusive civil society that alone mobilises the talents, energies and co-operation of the population to create a modern industrial society.[52]

Note that nationalisms of which Kerevan disapproves (not least because they threaten to discredit his own nationalism by association) are dismissed as mere 'tribalism'. Conversely, 'civic' nationalism is with equal frequency presented as not really being a form of nationalism at all. Only the 'tribalism' of Milosevic, which, as Michael Ignatieff puts it, 'legitimises an appeal to blood loyalty', is designated as such. In either event, the desired effect is to protect 'civic' nationalism from any suggestion that it appeals to blood and soil.[53] Marxists do distinguish between different forms of nationalism, in particular between those of oppressors and oppressed, but this is not what is being argued here.[54] What is interesting about the argument about 'civic' nationalism is that it is precisely the one that has historically been used to defend multinational oppressor nationalisms like those of Britain and the US.

During the Scottish parliamentary elections of May 1999 *The Daily Record* issued a warning to its readers that the nationalism of the Scottish National Party could lead to the type of brutality exercised by the Serbs against the Kosovan Albanians. Here the British nationalism supported by both *The Daily Record* and its party of choice, the British Labour Party, simply disappears from view, despite the fact that it has been used to mobilise support for actual, as opposed to hypothetical, bloodletting for nearly 300 years and has recently been doing so again in the Balkans. The notion that British nationalism is not 'really' nationalism at all is of course a venerable theme of ruling class ideologues. It was first systematically expressed by the historian Lord Acton in an article of 1862 where he argued that the multinational character of the British nation ensured that 'freedom' (in the economic sense understood by mid-Victorian liberals) was secure: 'The combination of different nations in one state is as necessary a condition of civilised life as the combination of men in society.' One of the benefits conferred by this arrangement was that the 'intellectually superior' would elevate 'inferior races' hitherto corrupted by despotism or democracy. How different this beneficent fusion was to the situation elsewhere in Europe: 'Where political and national boundaries coincide, society ceases to advance, and nations relapse into a condition corresponding to that of men who renounce intercourse with their fellow men'.[55]

This analysis, or second or third hand versions of it, clearly informs the attitude of contemporary supporters of the British state, such as Gordon Brown, who are happy to dwell on their abhorrence of Scottish nationalism while simultaneously offering their support for British bombers whose sides are decorated with the Union Jack. Social psychologist Michael Billig has characterised the everyday nationalism of the established imperial states as 'banal nationalism': '"Our" nationalism is not presented as nationalism, which is dangerously irrational, surplus and alien.' Other people have nationalism; at best, 'we' have patriotism. Billig aims his comments specifically at the situation in the US, but they have a broader applicability: 'The wars waged by US troops; the bombing in Vietnam and Iraq; the bombast of successive US presidents; and the endless display of the revered flag; all of these are removed from the problems of overheated nationalism'.[56] As these comments suggest, there are significant difficulties for socialists in attempting to use 'civic' nationalism as an alternative to 'ethnic' nationalism. Two in particular stand out.

The first is that the category of the 'civic' avoids any engagement with the fact that there are certain activities which nation states must undertake, regardless of how non-ethnic they may be. As Billig complains, Ignatieff 'does not describe how "civic nationalists" create a nation-state with its own myths; how the civic nations recruit their citizenry in wartime; how they draw their boundaries; how they demarcate "others" behind those boundaries; how they resist, violently if necessary, those movements which seek to rearrange the boundaries; and so on.'

The second is that, as we have seen, ethnicities can be invented to categorise groups by their enemies, or as self identification by those groups themselves, without any reference to real or imaginary kinship relations: culture can just as easily be made the basis of ethnicity as blood and soil tribalism. Precisely because ethnicity is a socially constructed category, however, ethnic categorisations can be produced anywhere with the same disastrous results that we have seen for the last ten years in the Balkans. Consequently there is no reason why 'civic' nationalism cannot be transformed into 'ethnic' nationalism in its turn under certain determinate conditions, just as it was in Germany—a modern, developed and highly cultured capitalist society—during the 1930s.[57] This is a conclusion that adherents of 'civic' nationalism are, of course, most anxious to avoid.

The example of Scotland is worth considering in this context for two reasons: first, because the historical record demonstrates how even this most civil of societies first rose on a sea of ethnic blood; second, because the contemporary situation contains all the elements for an 'ethnic' nationalism to arise—and in this Scotland is no different from most other Western European nations, although it tends to evade the scrutiny to which English nationalism is rightly subject.

The modern Scottish nation was created through two processes: first, the destruction of the Highland society and the incorporation of its imagery into the national self image; second, the consolidation of that image through participation in the conquest and colonisation of North America and India. Both processes included ferocious episodes of what we would now call 'ethnic cleansing'.

The Highlanders were considered to be no better than the Catholic Irish—indeed, their language and persons were often described in this way in both the Lowlands and England. One self proclaimed 'gentleman' of Derby, who had Highlanders quartered on him during the Jacobite occupation of that town in 1745, expressed every existing prejudice possible about the Highlanders in the space of one brief letter. First was their appearance: 'Most of the men, after their entrance into my house, looked like so many fiends turned out of hell to ravage the kingdom and cut throats; and under their plaids nothing but various sorts of butchering weapons were to be seen.' Even though these fiends in human form proceeded to eat and drink this gentleman out of house and home (although unaccountably failing to cut either his throat or those of his family), he could still find amusement in their religious observance: 'What did afford me some matter for an unavoidable laughter (though my family was in a miserable condition) was to see these desperadoes, from officers to the common men, at their several meals, first pull off their bonnets, and then lift up their eyes in a most solemn manner, and mutter something to themselves, by way of saying grace—as if they had been so many primitive Christians.' As if, indeed. His greatest abuse, however, is reserved for their language: 'Their dialect (from the idea I had of it) seemed to me as if a herd of Hottentots, wild monkeys in a desert or vagrant Gypsies had been jabbering, screaming, and howling together; and really this jargon of speech was very suited to such a set of banditti'.[58] The conflation of 'Hottentot', 'monkey' and 'Gypsy' is suggestive and horrifying, but no different from what was commonly said about the Irish. And this is how they were treated in the aftermath of the Battle of Culloden. Discussing the brutality shown to the defeated Scottish Highlanders by the British army, the historian Alan Macinnes has written that the actions of the victorious Hanoverian troops involved 'systematic state terrorism, characterised by a genocidal intent that verged on "ethnic cleansing".'[59] At the forefront of these atrocities were the Lowland Scots.

As the warrior vanguard of British imperialism, however, the Highlanders behaved no better than the Lowlanders or the English. The Native Americans, to whom the Highlanders have been so frequently and inaccurately compared, might have expected different treatment at their hands than was generally dispensed by settlers from elsewhere in the British Isles. Alas, this was not the case. There were individual examples of intermarriage, or even of Highlanders adopting Native American lifestyles, but as James Hunter writes, 'Most North American Indian native peoples...would have been hard pressed to distinguish between the behaviour of Scottish Highlanders or any other of the various types of European with whom they came into contact.' In some cases this behaviour contained some particularly bitter ironies: 'Emigrants to Cape Breton Island, many of them refugees from clearances...showed not the slightest scruple about displacing the area's traditional inhabitants, the Micmac, from territories the latter had occupied for much longer than there had been Gaelic speaking Scots in Scotland'.[60] Scotland was of course itself an imperial power, or, as an integral part of the British state, at least a major component of one. We are fortunate to have an excellent description of imperial rule in Asia by

James Callender, a Scottish radical active during the 1780s and 1790s:

In Bengal only, we destroyed or expelled within the short period of six years no less than five million industrious and harmless people; and as we have been sovereigns in that country for about 35 years, it may be reasonably computed that we have strewn the plains of Indostan with 15 or 20 million carcasses... The persons positively destroyed must, in whole, have exceeded 20 million, or 2,000...acts of homicide per annum. These victims have been sacrificed to the balance of power, and the balance of trade, the honour of the British flag.[61]

Nor is the type of racism associated with empire something of the distant past. As late as 1923 a committee of the Church of Scotland, asked to consider the effects of Irish immigration to Scotland, produced a report to the General Assembly in which the Catholic Irish were described as 'a people by themselves, segregated by reason of their race, their customs, their traditions, and, above all, by their loyalty to their church'. The Scottish and Irish 'races' could never mix, or even live together, because:

The Irish are the most obedient children of the Church of Rome; the Scots stubbornly adhere to the principles of the reformed faith [Protestantism]. *The Irish have separate schools for their children; they have their own clubs for recreation and social intercourse; they tend to segregate in communities, and even to monopolise certain departments of labour to the exclusion of Scots.*[62]

It should be obvious, therefore, that it is historically inaccurate to claim that the Scottish nation has had a purely 'civic' national identity, and it is politically myopic to imagine that a full blown 'ethnic' nationalism could not re-emerge here under certain conditions. The materials are there in the traditions of Protestant sectarianism, militarism, or even simply 'whiteness'. On the latter point it is worth noting that the Commission for Racial Equality reported in May 1999 that Scotland had 1,087 recorded racial incidents during 1997-1998, compared to 441 in Wales and 13,437 in England. Although Scotland is home to only 2.1 per cent of 'ethnic minorities' in Britain, it recorded 7.3 per cent of all racially motivated incidents. In central Scotland, where the majority of incidents were reported, the percentage was 15 times higher than in central London. None of these remarks are intended to contribute to *The Daily Record* style hysteria about Scottish nationalism. The chances of an ethnic national movement arising in the near future strike me as unlikely, and the Scottish National Party is equally unlikely to be a vehicle for such a nationalism should it arise, but it is necessary to remind ourselves that there are no nations on earth, be their nationalisms ever so 'civic', where 'ethnic' divisions could not be invented and 'cleansing' imposed if the material conditions were right.

Conclusion

It could be argued that I am displaying too great a concern with mere terminology and, given the way in which the academic left is currently obsessed with language, this would be an understandable response. Nevertheless, the dire political consequences that have previously followed the widespread adoption of certain terms ('patriarchy', for example) tend to suggest that terminological shifts not only register changed ways of thinking, but also encourage such changes. As the Russian Marxist Valentin Voloshinov wrote, 'The word is the most sensitive index of social changes', and if, as Voloshinov also suggests, the word is 'an arena of class struggle', then it is high time that we began to wage it over the word 'ethnicity'.[63]

In his recent book on culture, Adam Kuper concludes with sentiments that are equally relevant to the discussion of ethnicity:

> ...*unless we separate out the various processes that are lumped together under the heading of culture, and look beyond the field of culture to other processes, then we will not get very far in understanding any of it. For the same sort of reason, cultural identity can never provide an adequate guide for living. We all have multiple identities, and even if I accept that I have a primary cultural identity, I may not want to conform to it. Besides, it may not be very practical. I operate in the market, live through my body, struggle in the grip of others. If I am to regard myself only as a cultural being, I allow myself very little room to manoeuvre, or to question the world in which I find myself.*

Kuper notes that there is a final objection to defining ourselves in this way, which he describes as 'moral', but which is actually political: 'It tends to draw attention away from what we have in common instead of encouraging us to communicate across national, ethnic and religious boundaries, and to venture between them'.[64] Although rendered in liberal individualistic terms, this is well said. For socialists, the aim is to overcome the divisions which are increasingly described as 'ethnic' by removing the oppressions that give them significance, not to perpetuate or add to them. This may mean supporting oppressed nations or peoples, but the notion of 'ethnicity' is ultimately a means of dividing people up into ever more arbitrary classifications. At best, under the guise of celebrating 'cultural difference', it only obscures what most working people, which is most people, have in common by emphasising relatively super-ficial aspects of our social world. At worst, in a struggle for scarce resources such as that currently being played out in the Balkans, it can be used as a means of marking down certain people for persecution. As I have tried to suggest, there is no reason why we in Britain should feel complacent about the implications of 'ethnic cleansing' for ourselves. The necessary elements of 'ethnicity' can always be assembled from whatever historical relics are lying around, if economic crisis and social collapse are sufficiently severe. The anthropologist Marcus Banks wrote recently of ethnicity: 'Unfortunately...it is too late to kill it off or pro-nounce ethnicity dead; the discourse on ethnicity has escaped from the academy and into the field'.[65] This is too pessimistic. To dispense with the concept, we must first dispense with the social conditions that require the thing to which it refers, but it is possible to make a start. To para-phrase Alasdair MacIntyre in another context, understanding the uses to which 'ethnicity' has been put leads comprehensively to the conclusion that it is a term which no honest person should continue to use.[66]

Notes

This article is based on a talk given at the 'Why Is NATO Bombing Yugoslavia?' conference organised by the Edinburgh Campaign Against War In Europe and held at the University of Edinburgh on 23 May 1999. Thanks to Margaret MacDonald, Laura Mitchell and Gerry Mooney for helpful comments.

1   M Banks, *Ethnicity: Anthropological Constructions* (London and New York, 1996), pp167-168; 'Notes and Queries', *The Guardian*, 17 June 1999. The first area to be 'cleansed' in this way seems to have been the Croat village of Kijevo in the otherwise Serb dominated province of Krajina during August 1991. See L Silber and A Little, *The Death Of Yugoslavia* (Harmondsworth, 1995), pp188-190.

2   See, for example, M Mann, 'The Dark Side of Democracy: the Modern Tradition of Ethnic and Political Cleansing', *New Left Review* 235 (May-June 1999), pp31-32, 42-43.

3   V I Lenin, 'What Is To Be Done?', *Selected Works*, vol 1 (Moscow, 1975), p145.

4   P L van den Berghe, 'Race and Ethnicity: a Sociobiological Perspective', *Ethnic and Racial Studies*, vol 1, no 4 (October 1978), p404.

5   S Reynolds, 'Medieval Origines Gentium and the Community of the Realm', *History*, vol 68, no 224 (October 1983), p379.

6   L Colley, *Britons* (London, 1992), p15.

7   M Lynch, *Scotland: A New History* (Revised Edition, London, 1992), p12. The origins of this process were famously mocked in the deathless prose of Sellar and Yeatman: 'The Scots (originally Irish, but by now Scotch) were this time inhabiting Ireland, having driven the Irish (Picts) out of Scotland; while the Picts (originally Scots) were now Irish (living in brackets) and vice versa. It is essential to keep these distinctions clearly in mind (and vice versa).' W C Sellar and R J Yeatman, *1066 And All That* (Harmondsworth, 1960), p13.

8   S Rose, L J Kamin and R C Lewontin, *Not In Our Genes* (Harmondsworth, 1984), p126.

9   E R Wolf, *Europe And The Peoples Without History* (Berkeley and Los Angeles, 1982), p71.

10   The Catholic Irish are discussed below. For a brief discussion of how increasing social differences between Lowland and Highland Scotland led the inhabitants of the former region to regard those of the latter as a distinct 'race' or 'ethnicity', see N Davidson, 'Scotland's Bourgeois Revolution', in C Bambery (ed), *Scotland, Class and Nation* (London, 1999), pp58-61, 120-121.

11   E R Wolf, op cit, pp380, 381.

12   The third group, the Twas, are pygmies and consequently physically distinct from the other two, but in any event they comprised only 1 percent of the population at the time of colonisation.

13   C Kimber, 'Coming to Terms With Barbarism in Rwanda and Burundi', *International Socialism* 73 (Winter 1996), pp128-129.

14   T H Eriksen, *Ethnicity and Nationalism* (London and Chicago, 1993), pp87-88.

15   Ibid, p82.

16   'The surest sign that a society has entered into the secure possession of a new concept', writes Quentin Skinner, 'is that a new vocabulary will be developed in terms of which the concept can then be publicly articulated and discussed.' He takes the example of how the term 'state' emerged during the Reformation to describe 'a form of public power separate from both the ruler and the ruled, and constituting a supreme political authority within a certain defined territory'. Yet the state existed for thousands of years before the word came into use. Q Skinner, *The Foundations Of Modern Political Thought*, vol 2 (Cambridge, 1978), pp351-354.

17   A D Smith, *National Identity* (Harmondsworth, 1991), p21.

18   Ibid, p14.

19   T H Erickson, op cit, p3. Their usage has clear affinities with the notion of a 'status group' introduced by Max Weber to describe differentiation at the social level, as opposed to occupational 'class' at the economic and 'party' interest at the political. See M Weber, 'Class, Status, Party', in H H Gerth and C Wright Mills (eds), *From Max Weber: Essays In Sociology* (London, 1948), pp186-194. Weber was sceptical about the usefulness of 'ethnicity' as a means of describing identity and tended to use the term more to describe the character of endogamous groups. For an example of this see, for example, 'Structures of Power', ibid, p173. It should be noted that under Stalinism the notion of 'ethnicity' was also put to work in similarly ideological ways. During the Brezhnev period in particular a group of Soviet anthropologists, the most important of whom was Yulian Bromley, developed a theory of *ethnos* which claimed that the constituent peoples of the republic retained an ethnic identity which had continuity throughout the feudal, capitalist and socialist epochs. The function of this theory, whose anti-Marxist content went some way to ensuring it a relatively friendly reception in the West, was to explain why various national characteristics of, say, the Armenians, had failed to wither away under 'socialism', by reference to an trans-historical 'ethnicity'. At the same time the celebration of various 'ethnicities' could be used as a covert way of allowing the subject peoples of the Stalinist Empire a means of cultural expression without threatening the integrity of the state. For relatively sympathetic accounts of these theories, see M Banks, op cit, pp17-24; T Shanin, 'Soviet Theories of Ethnicity: the Case of a Missing Term', *New Left Review* 158 (July-August 1986), pp118-122. John Foster, one of the few Stalinist in Britain to retain a respect for the outpourings of the Soviet Academy right till the end, attempted to put these theories of *ethnos* into effect with respect to Scotland in several articles where he claimed that Scottish nationhood was first formed during the feudal epoch. Such positions are of course standard among the nationalists who march to Bannockburn every year to celebrate the victory of the Scottish 'nation' over Edward II in 1314, although they have managed to reach

this position without the assistance of Bromley et al. See, in particular, J Foster, 'Nationality, Social Change and Class: Transformations of National Identity in Scotland', in D McCrone, S Kendrick and P Straw (eds), *The Making of Scotland: Nation, Culture and Social Change* (Edinburgh, 1989), p40.

20   M Banks, op cit, p72. Banks suggests that the rise of Nazi Germany was a reason why Germans made less of their origins than, for example, Poles, but the 'assimilationist' nature of German immigrants was well established long before 1933.

21   L Carroll, 'Through the Looking Glass and What Alice Found There', in *The Penguin Complete Lewis Carroll* (Harmondsworth, 1982), p196.

22   S Hall, 'Brave New World', *Marxism Today*, vol 32, no 10 (October 1988), p29.

23   A Cohen, *Two-Dimensional Man* (London, 1974), p15.

24   No Sizwe (N Alexander), *One Azania, One Nation* (London, 1978), p137. Max Weber made the same point, in more academic language, much earlier in the century: 'All in all, the notion of "ethnically" determined social action subsumes phenomena that a rigorous sociological analysis...would have to distinguish carefully... It is certain that in this process the collective term "ethnic" would be abandoned, for it is unsuitable for a really rigorous analysis.' And in the next paragraph Weber describes how the 'concept of the ethnic group...dissolves if we define our terms exactly'. See M Weber, *Economy And Society,* vol 1 (Berkeley and Los Angeles, 1968), p395.

25   S Hall, 'Our Mongrel Selves', *New Statesman and Society*, 19 June 1992, p6.

26   S Hall, 'The New Ethnicities', J Hutchinson and A D Smith (eds), op cit, p163.

27   J Hutchinson and A D Smith (eds), Preface, op cit, pv.

28   T H Eriksen, op cit, pp13-14.

29   M Cross, 'Colonialism and Ethnicity: a Theory and Comparative Case Study', *Ethnic And Racial Studies*, vol 1, no 1 (January 1978), p40.

30   D Brown, 'Why is the Nation-State so Vulnerable to Ethnic Nationalism?', *Nations And Nationalism*, vol 4, no 1 (January 1998), p13.

31   A Kuper, *Culture: The Anthropologist's Account* (London and Cambridge, Massachusetts, 1999), pp238-239. Kuper is South African and correctly describes himself as a liberal. Like that other exiled son of the British dominions, the Australian Robert Hughes in *The Culture Of Complaint*, he treads a fine line between acute commentary on follies of much 'radical' thought and a dismissal of the problems it seeks to address.

32   D Brown, op cit, p13.

33   M Glenny, *The Fall Of Yugoslavia* (Harmondsworth, 1992), pp141-142.

34   A Bell-Fialkoff, 'A Brief History of Ethnic Cleansing', *Foreign Affairs*, vol 72, no 3 (July 1993), p121.

35   E J Hobsbawm, 'Ethnicity and Nationalism in Europe Today', in G Balakrishnan (ed), *Mapping the Nation* (London and New York, 1996), p260.

36   A Sivanandan, 'R[ace] A[wareness] T[raining] and the Degradation of Black Struggle', *Communities of Resistance* (London and New York, 1990), p94.

37   S Fenton, *Ethnicity: Racism, Class and Culture* (Houndmills, 1999), p69.

38   See P Alexander, *Racism, Resistance and Revolution* (London, 1987), ch 1.

39   M Barker, *The New Racism* (London, 1981), pp4-5.

40   T W Allan, *The Invention Of The White Race*, vol 1 (London and New York, 1994), pp14-21, 32, 48, 65-66, 77-79, 92. The second volume of this important work has yet to appear.

41   A Kuper, op cit, ppxii-xiii.

42   The Race Relations Act 1976, S.3 (1), (2).

43   H Ousley, Preface, Commission for Racial Equality, *Racial Equality Means Quality* (London, 1995), p5.

44   No Sizwe, op cit, p137.

45   A Callinicos, *Race And Class* (London, 1993), pp32-33.

46   M Barker, op cit, p5.

47   In fact, many members of the Communication Workers Union refused to deliver Nazi election material, but not, alas, those delivering to Edinburgh postal district EH6.

48   T Nairn, 'Does Tomorrow Belong to the Bullets or the Bouquets?', *New Statesman And Society*, 19 June 1992, p31. For similar arguments, couched within an explicit appeal to sociobiology, see P L van den Berghe, op cit.

49   B Rolston, 'Culture as a Battlefield: Political Identity and the State in the North of Ireland', *Race And Class*, vol 39, no 4 (April-June 1998), pp28-30.

50   A Kuper, op cit, pp238-239.

51   J G Kellas, *The Politics Of Nationalism And Ethnicity* (Houndmills, 1998), p65.

52   G Kerevan, 'Milosevic's "Nationalism" Is Not Ours', *The Scotsman*, 5 April 1999. Compare Lord Acton in 1862: 'These two views of nationality, corresponding to the French and English systems, are connected in name only, and are in reality the opposite extremes of political thought.' Lord Acton, 'Nationality', in G Balakrishnan (ed), op cit, p29.

53   M Ignatieff, *Blood And Belonging* (London, 1993), p6.

54   See N Davidson, 'In Perspective: Tom Nairn', *International Socialism* 82 (Spring 1999), pp124-125, and A Callinicos, 'Marxism and the National Question', in C Bambery (ed), op cit.

55   Lord Acton, op cit, p31.

56   M Billig, *Banal Nationalism* (London, 1995), pp55, 57.

57   See N Davidson, 'In Perspective: Tom Nairn', op cit, p113; D Gluckstein, *The Nazis, Capitalism And The Working Class* (London, 1999), ch 1.

58   'Extract of a Letter from a Gentleman at Derby', *The Gentleman's Magazine and Historical Chronicle*, vol 16 (January 1746), p16.

59   A I Macinnes, *Clanship, Commerce and the House of Stuart, 1603-1788* (East Linton, 1996), p211. See also p32. On p215 the Hanoverian High Command is no longer described as having a policy 'verging' on 'ethnic cleansing', but of 'opting' for it without qualification.

60   J Hunter, *A Dance Called America* (Edinburgh, 1994), p237. Hunter recounts one of the more positive encounters between the Highland Scots and the Native Americans, in this case the MacDonalds of Glencoe and the Nez Perce, in his *Glencoe and the Indians* (Edinburgh, 1996).

61   J T Callender, *The Political Progress of Great Britain; or an Impartial Account of the Principal Abuses in the Government of this Country from the Revolution in 1688* (Edinburgh, 1792), pp1-2.

62   'Report of Committee to Consider Overtures from the Presbytery of Glasgow and from the Synod of Glasgow and Ayr on Irish Immigrants and the Education (Scotland) Act 1918', 29 May 1923 (Edinburgh, 1923); 'Report on the Schemes of the Church of Scotland with Legislative Acts Passed by the General Assembly' (Edinburgh, 1923), pp750, 760-761. Some academics such as Steven Bruce have argued that this was an unrepresentative committee 'whose views and enthusiasm were not shared by the majority'. The key, according to Bruce, is that the church lacked the willingness to act (see S Bruce, 'Sectarianism in Scotland: a Contemporary Assessment and Explanation', D McCrone and A Brown (eds), *The Scottish Government Yearbook 1988* (Edinburgh, 1988), p165, n25). In fact the membership of the committee included both the Moderator and the Procurator, the leading officials of the Church of Scotland.

63   V N Voloshinov, *Marxism And The Philosophy Of Language* (London and Cambridge, Massachusetts, 1986), pp19, 23.

64   A Kuper, op cit, p247.

65   M Banks, op cit, p189.

66   A MacIntyre, ' "Ought",' *Against the Self-Images of the Age* (London, 1971), p156.

Class struggles in France

JIM WOLFREYS

The tide turns: class struggle, fascism and the left in France[1]

'Don't you think', the newscaster asked prime minister Lionel Jospin, 'that there's a whiff of a pre-May 1968 or a pre-revolutionary situation in the air?'[2] Certainly, on this particular day in January 1998, two years after the great public sector strikes of December 1995, the combativity of French workers was showing little sign of abating. The events of that December had been followed by a series of successful strikes by tram-workers;[3] a high profile campaign by immigrants seeking residence papers (*sans-papiers*) which culminated in the occupation of a Paris church in the summer of 1996; a militant strike by lorry drivers the following autumn; the occupation, in January 1997, of the Credit Foncier bank by 2,000 employees protesting against its closure; a massive and confident demonstration against plans to reinforce racist anti-immigration legislation in February; a magnificent 50,000 strong march on the National Front (FN) congress in Strasbourg a month later; a second lorry drivers' strike the following November; and then, before, during and after Christmas in the winter of 1997-1998, weeks of protests and occupations by associations of the unemployed which thrust the demand for more state aid for those out of work to the centre of political debate.

Television news pictures showed angry demonstrators striding into well to do restaurants and demanding to be given food. When one group was offered an out of the way table in the basement they stood firm until they were seated alongside the other diners. Jospin found himself obliged to appear on the evening news to put the government's case. The format of his interview revealed how the mood in France had shifted. Before anything was asked of him, Jospin was made to sit through two interviews with unemployed workers. 'If he says, "There you are, here's a £150 [a month] raise in benefits", he's going to solve nothing,' one of them warned Jospin. 'He's got to get that into his head'.[4] Each time concessions were won from the government, the impression that Jospin, whom protesters compared to a piggy bank, could be made to give way again, grew—a feeling neatly summed up by one trade unionist who told the *Libération* newspaper, 'We're going to carry on shaking the little piggy from Cintegabelle'.[5]

Still the protests did not let up. On a bright spring day in March 1998 tens of thousands of demonstrators gathered in Paris to march from the Bastille to the Place de la Nation against the National Front. Many anti-FN protests had followed the same route during the 15 years since the party's emergence as a major political force. But this one was different. Whereas in the early 1990s demonstrations tended to be defensive, bitter affairs,[6] anti-racist protests by the end of the decade had become a vibrant, heady mix of combativity and optimism. The imprint on the march of the so called social movement that had first exploded in December 1995[7] was everywhere: in the manifest confidence of those present, in the slogans and banners (one read simply, 'Watch out, here comes the spring'), and in the presence of contingents of revitalised anti-racist organisations and striking teachers from the Seine-Saint-Denis region to the north of Paris, in dispute with the Socialist education minister Claude Allègre. Throughout 1998 and into 1999 the struggles have continued, with teachers, medical staff, pilots, the unemployed and immigrants continuing to mobilise against Jospin's left coalition government elected in June 1997. In October 1998 school students, angry at the lack of teachers and resources, at their own workload, at overcrowded classrooms and at the state of school buildings, took to the streets. A wave of protests erupted across France. In a single week over a million school students demonstrated in over 350 towns.[8]

The revival of the labour movement during the 1990s has had implications for the whole of the political spectrum. On the right, the question of how to confront this resurgence has led to a polarisation between those seeking confrontation and those opting for compromise. All three major right wing parties—the Gaullist Rassemblement pour la République (RPR), the centre-right Union pour la Démocratie Française (UDF) and the fascist National Front (FN)—put on the defensive since 1995, have suffered splits and resignations. On the left the Socialist Party (PS) has resurrected its reformist credentials, the Communist Party

(PCF) is shedding its Stalinist image in an attempt to redefine itself as a mainstream social democratic party, while the Greens and the Trotskyist left have found a significant electoral audience. What follows is an analysis of the unfolding crisis of French society which centres on the different forces attempting to set the political agenda. It begins with an assessment of the resurgence of class struggle before examining its political implications, focusing on the labour movement, the record of the left coalition in office and the recent split in the National Front. The article ends with an assessment of how France's Trotskyist left has responded to the new situation.

The lessons of December

Towards the end of 1967, unaware that within months the biggest general strike in France's history would all but end his presidency, Charles de Gaulle declared, 'I greet the year 1968 with serenity...with satisfaction'.[9] Jacques Chirac, leader of the Gaullist RPR, could have been forgiven for similar complacency as he surveyed the political scene in 1994 and prepared for his presidential campaign. The right held over 80 percent of seats in the National Assembly, the Socialist Party had been reduced to a rudderless rump, winning only 14 percent of the vote in the 1994 European election, and Chirac's friend and ally, prime minister Edouard Balladur, was riding high in the polls. Chirac seemed to have seen off the threat to his authority from within his own party, both from the so called 'fortysomething' reformers, many of whom were now under investigation for corruption, and from the orthodox Gaullists, the reactionary Charles Pasqua and the more moderate Philippe Séguin, who had formed an unholy anti-Chirac alliance in the early 1990s.

Chirac, however, had counted without the personal ambition of Balladur, who repudiated 30 years of friendship and an alleged agreement between the two men to declare himself a candidate for the presidency. Since Balladur had staked his campaign on his government's record of economic liberalism, Chirac's only chance, given the parlous state of the Socialists, would be to outflank Balladur on the left. This strategy was a risky one since Chirac not only had a reputation as being uncompromisingly right wing (as a government representative in negotiations with the CGT trade union in May 1968 he is rumoured to have gone into talks with a revolver stuffed in his belt),[10] but was also responsible for the RPR's 'liberal turn' of the mid-1980s when he turned his back on the protectionist, state-directed legacy of de Gaulle and embraced the free market.[11] Chirac's attitude to the 1995 campaign was breezily dishonest: 'I will astonish you', he told his advisers, 'with my demagogy'.[12] Aided by Séguin, he drew up a manifesto which promised

'a France for all', and made the central theme of his campaign the 'social
fracture' which had divided the country into haves and have nots. His
strategy was based on the political calculation that the haughty and aristocratic demeanour of Balladur would appear remote and out of touch
alongside his own earthy populism.[13] But the campaign also struck a
chord because the 'social fracture' was a reality.[14] Having defeated
Balladur and the Socialist Party candidate, Lionel Jospin, who managed
to revive the PS vote and even win the first round ballot, Chirac
appointed Alain Juppé prime minister. When it became clear that Juppé,
an aloof, calculating technocrat, memorably described by a Socialist
deputy as the 'personification of tax', had absolutely no intention of
addressing France's social crisis, an almighty backlash ruined Juppé's
career and effectively scuppered the Chirac presidency too.

The backlash came in the form of massive public sector strikes in
December 1995 against the swingeing cuts which Juppé proposed for the
social security system. The implementation of the Juppé Plan was itself
an illustration of the uncertainty gripping the right over how to curb state
spending and deal with opposition to the cutbacks. The concessions
offered by Balladur in the face of protests during his premiership earned
him the nickname 'Ballamou' (*mou* meaning soft as opposed to *dur*
meaning hard). When Alain Madelin advocated taking an uncompromising hard line he was sacked from the Juppé government. Yet within
months Juppé was waging an onslaught of his own. For several weeks
two million public sector workers brought France's cities to a virtual
standstill and hundreds of thousands of workers took part in the biggest
demonstrations seen since May 1968. The strikes were initiated by the
trade union leadership:

> *But from a very early point on the movement began to break out of the usual
> bureaucratic confines. It displayed the spontaneous militancy, combativity
> and growing class consciousness which Rosa Luxemburg emphasised [in **The
> Mass Strike, the Political Party and the Trade Unions**]. It did so because it
> gave expression to the enormous bitterness towards existing rulers, bosses
> and institutions that is characteristic of the popular mood in the 1990s right
> across the advanced countries. In a very real sense it was a product of those
> features that differentiate the 1990s from the 1980s.*[15]

One journalist, present one evening at two impromptu mass meetings
at a postal depot in Paris, described how the strike spread like 'a powder
trail'.[16] Striking railway workers called on the postal workers to join
them: 'We can win but we need numbers. We are going to paralyse the
economy. We have to get round other workplaces and explain to people.'

The more time passed, the more the idea of a general strike warmed the spirits. The need is to act quickly, get ahead of the game, win over other depots. And why not 'Auster' (Austerlitz), on the other side of the Seine? Led by the railway workers, the troop is off again, across the railway tracks...to the cry of 'Auster join us!'... [a] third mass meeting is improvised... [and] won over by the arguments of a young activist in blue overalls: 'In the private sector it's more difficult to fight. We must fight for the conditions of the whole working class, the public sector, the private sector and the unemployed.' Thunderous applause. 'Auster' is won over. Already the talk is of the next conquest. [17]

Across Paris at the Gare du Nord station someone wrote, 'No, the Commune is not dead!' on the walls. Day after day the press and TV were filled with images of strikers and demonstrations. The RPR's attempts to form anti-strike 'consumers' committees' were an abject failure. One group of strikers was watching a local news broadcast which went live to an RPR meeting. They immediately rushed down to the venue and bricked up the door to the building! Karl Marx was voted 'man of the year' by a national newspaper.[18] 'I was dreaming of this,' said one railway worker, 'a mini-revolution. I'm up to my neck in debt but I don't care. I've stopped counting. We're all together. We're not giving up'.[19]

The strikes represented a huge slap in the face for every professional sociologist who had argued that the working class was a spent force: 'They wanted to throw class struggle out through the door, it came back in through the window'.[20] One group of influential academics, having published a petition in defence of the government's attack on public services,[21] then proceeded to develop an analysis which sought to belittle the significance of the strikes. They were 'defensive', 'backward looking', 'corporatist', 'irrational', a 'one-off'. An article in *Le Monde*, disgracefully, even tried to insinuate a comparison between the strikes and National Front ideology.[22] Even the term 'social movement', which is now commonly used to describe the continuing strike wave, is a euphemism which implies that it is fundamentally apolitical in character. The academic mainstream still clings to its dismissal of class. In a book published in 1996 two prominent sociologists summed up the main thrust of the argument:

In the absence of any positive representation of progress, the maintenance of the status quo and the defence of 'established gains' carry the day. There is, moreover, no real collective action in the real sense of the term, which is to say action producing solidarity and social change. There remain only an addition of individual or sectional defence mechanisms, making the generalisation of demands, that go with a class logic, impossible. [23]

The reality, as we shall see, could not have been more different. What began as a public sector strike against the Juppé government's plans to reform the social security system sparked a sea change in French politics, creating a new mood characterised by a backlash against free market economics, a belief that strikes work, and widespread rejection of the scapegoating of immigrants and the stigmatising of the unemployed. In short, 1995 marked the end of a 'period of resignation',[24] and an end to the liberal consensus of the 1980s, ultimately posing the question about 'what kind of society we live in and want to live in'.[25]

A decade and a half of recession and austerity had had a cumulative effect. In some cases it led to profound despondency, reflected in the following remarks by a supermarket cashier:

> *Work here is slavery, we're humiliated; work...doesn't mean anything anymore. We get just enough to survive. No point even thinking about plans for the future. As for me, I ask myself how I ever thought I was going to do something with my life.*[26]

The appalling record of the left in office, discussed below, had robbed many of any sense that an alternative way of living was possible. But cynicism about political representatives cut both ways. In the early 1990s increasing numbers began to take things into their own hands. Air France workers struck successfully in 1993 and the following year school students forced the Balladur government to back down on its plans to introduce a cheap youth employment scheme. Early in 1994 an article in *Le Monde* described France's social climate as poised 'between resignation and explosion'.[27] Going by the bald statistics of the time the prospects for struggle looked bleak. Union membership was falling,[28] and, from an average of around three million a year in the 1970s, the annual total of strike days had dropped to below half a million in the 1990s.[29] But the explosion happened. Those involved in the strikes underlined again and again their cathartic effect. 'Instead of making the trains work, we made ideas work',[30] was one railway worker's memory of December. 'Strikes', argued a Paris Metro worker, 'completely change a man':

> *People live in their own little corner. They come first, never mind their neighbour... During the strikes individualism was completely 'broken up'. Completely! The chains were broken! Spontaneously. Because we were discussing things all the time, we learned to get to know each other. We were at the firm 24 hours a day. In our job we're very isolated and we only see each other during the ten minute breaks. Here we learned to live together.*[31]

Suddenly the possibilities for real change came alive. A nurse involved in the strikes told how, having dropped out of political activity, her ideas had been turned around:

If I felt concerned again it's because this time it was about essential demands, political... It was the rejection of a capitalist society, the rejection of money. People were mobilised more against that than against the Juppé social security plan... At the end of the demos, people stayed where they were, as if they were waiting for something else.[32]

Far from being a corporatist or sectional revolt, the strikes of December 1995 were, in the words of one union delegate, 'a conflict of existence'.[33] Moreover, one of the defining features of the resurgence in class conflict has been the way in which links have been made, not just between different sections within particular industries, or even between different groups of workers, but between workers and almost every other group involved in struggle, from students and the unemployed to immigrants and gays. Sectionalism, which union activists had spent years trying to break down, suddenly began to disintegrate.[34] 'We are no longer fighting for ourselves,' one railway worker remarked a week into the 1995 strike:

...we are on strike for all wage earners. To start with I was on strike as a train driver, then as a railway worker, then as a public sector worker, and now it's as a wage earner that I'm on strike.[35]

The *coordination* movement and the role of the rank and file

Central to the solidarity that has underpinned the strikes of the past few years has been the ability of both rank and file union members and non-unionised workers to achieve greater democratic control over their actions. The strikes reflected a longstanding wariness of the trade union leadership. French unions are split along political lines into five main confederations and numerous smaller independent unions. The dominant union of the post-war period has been the Communist-dominated Confédération Générale du Travail (CGT), which survived a right wing split in 1947, leading to the formation of Force Ouvrière (FO), to play a key role in bringing the strikes of May 1968 to an end. In the wake of the May events the Confédération Française Démocratique du Travail (CFDT), formed in 1964, established itself as a younger, less dogmatic and more militant alternative to the CGT, more alive to feminism and ecological issues and, most importantly, to the new post-1968 buzzword, *autogestion,* or workers' 'self management', 'which could mean anything from full-blooded soviet power to a couple of union representatives on a consultative committee'.[36]

With the CGT suffering, along with the PCF, as a result both of the party's long term decline and of Communist participation in the first setbacks of the Mitterrand presidency, the 'realist' attitude adopted by the CFDT leadership during the 1980s, with the emphasis on concessions and negotiation rather than strike action, eventually provoked a reaction. Workers in several unions openly defied their leaders by taking strike action and turning their strike committees into *'coordinations'* which bypassed the bureaucracy. Between 1986 and 1988 strikes by railway and motor industry workers, students, postal workers, nurses and teachers were all led by autonomous *coordinations.* Some of them, like the nurses' Coordonner, Rassembler, Construire (CRC) and the postal workers SUD-PTT, became permanent structures, led by activists expelled from the CFDT. The attraction of the *coordinations*, particularly to young and non-unionised workers, was in their combativity and in their emphasis on unity and the democratic participation of the rank and file in union activity.

In numerous workplaces during December 1995 the mass meeting, lasting sometimes up to two hours, became the focal point for the strikes.[37] Strikers were conscious of the need to retain control over their representatives. 'For once', according to one commentator, 'the trade union rank and file was on the side of the active minority critical of the union leadership'.[38] Workers from elsewhere, and students, invited each other to take part in the meetings. Whereas before, strikes involving different groups of workers had appeared 'closed in on themselves', a new unity was emerging.[39] Another feature of the strikes was the involvement of young and non-unionised workers. One CGT representative for Paris transport workers recalls discussing with another union official, three or four days into the 1995 strike, whether to address political issues, only to find that 'we had already been overtaken by people who were neither politicised, members of an organisation, or unionised... They were mostly young, around 24 or 25 years old, who took up these issues in a very lively and very sharp way'.[40] According to one commentator, 'The traditional process whereby the conflict, in a kind of "raising of awareness", makes non-unionised workers discover trade union activism, was almost replaced by the exact opposite: the activists discovered their colleagues'.[41]

Confidence rekindled workers' pride and combativity, a palpable element in the massive demonstrations which filled the streets of every major French town and turned the air thick with the red flares of the railway workers. 'Before the conflict', declared one striker, 'I worked for the SNCF. Now I'm a railway worker'.[42] In Montpellier railway workers built tracks in the town centre.[43] Their counterparts in Paris, finding themselves stuck behind a slow moving contingent of electricity workers on one of the first demonstrations of 1995, streamed into the closed off section of the road and overtook them, saluting them with clenched fists and attempting to infect them with their dynamism, encouraging them to take up the slogan, 'Tous ensemble, tous ensemble'.[44]

This desire to spread the conflict and to learn from others in struggle has also been a distinguishing feature of the new mood. In 1996, when a group of so called *sans-papiers* (immigrants made 'illegal' by racist legislation introduced in 1994), occupied a Paris church, their demands became a national issue, inflamed by the decision of the Juppé government to send riot police in to smash down the doors with axes and evict the protesters. Subsequent protests by the unemployed have borrowed the tactic and occupied various prominent buildings, from job centres to the Bank of France, the Ecole Normale Supérieure and the Socialist Party headquarters. In 1996 a 5,000 strong protest against redundancies at a Moulinex factory in the town of Mamers took the form of a 'die-in', directly inspired by the AIDS awareness movement ACT-UP.[45] Also, as we have seen, the mass meetings of 1995 forged close links between workplaces, to the extent that the strikers were often more aware of what was happening elsewhere than the union leadership. In the eyes of one Paris Metro worker, 'This strike was directed by the rank and file, by the mass meetings. The union was not rejected, but its role was a logistical one of following up and carrying out collective decisions'.[46]

Such views nevertheless overestimate the extent of rank and file control and underestimate the ability of the trade union leadership to exert its influence, not least when it came to calling a halt to the movement. But the leadership was all the same forced to embrace elements of rank and file democracy in order to retain this influence, and to respect another major element in the 1995 strikes, the desire for unity, reflected in the number of joint union banners on the demonstrations and the fact that from the end of November there were no separate union contingents. Certainly the union leadership took the threat posed by the rank and file seriously. During the December strike wave no attempt was made to challenge the authority of mass meetings, and the CGT in particular made concerted efforts to generalise the movement to the private sector, staging an attempt, for example, to persuade the workforce at the Renault plant and Boulougne-Billancourt to support the railway workers.[47] But neither the CGT nor the Communist Party nor the Socialists offered a political lead to the movement. The slogan, 'Juppé, resign!' was never taken up by the representatives of the mainstream left. Indeed, on the demonstrations CGT representatives actively challenged those who did take up the slogan. Nor did the CGT draw up a list of general demands that could act as a rallying point for the whole movement, insisting instead on the need for sectional grievances to be dealt with first. When the government announced that it would hold a 'social summit' on the crisis and the question of ending the strike was posed, there was little effective opposition to the CGT's call to return to work.

In one railway depot on the outskirts of Paris the CGT ordered delegations from other workplaces (some of them invited by the CGT itself!) to leave the mass meeting which would vote on whether to end the strike, so that railway workers could decide 'among themselves'. CGT delegates proceeded to argue for a return to work, using the decision of a nearby depot of Metro workers to end their strike to support their argument. The workers, some of them in tears, voted to end their strike on the eve of a major demonstration. The following day Metro workers streamed into the depot to make an emotional appeal to continue the strike, having decided themselves to carry on. The CGT had lied to the meeting.[48]

The problem raised here concerns the best way to create an independent political alternative to the trade union leadership. The *coordinations*, which have been so much a feature of the struggles of the past decade or so, represent a powerful and democratic challenge to the bureaucracy. But their great strength is as an apparatus of struggle. In this sense they exist not so much as a subsititute for trade union organisation, but as a means of challenging the ability of the conservative bureaucracy to control strike action by providing a more democratic means of representing the wishes of the rank and file engaged in action.[49] The tendency to establish permanent structures based on the experience of the *coordinations* (often, it must be said, as a result of the expulsion of their leaders by the trade union leadership), is a different matter. On the one hand, the SUD (Solidaires, Unitaires, Démocratiques) unions have provided a channel for the most militant activists and an alternative to the conservative bureaucracy of the CFDT. On the other, however, their proliferation has divided an already fragmented trade union movement. The danger is that the best union activists, in their impatience to defy the bureaucracy, will isolate themselves from the main body of trade unionists and find themselves in radical and combative unions which organise only a tiny minority of workers. While this has not happened in the case of SUD-PTT, which has the support of around 15 percent of postal workers, there are now around a dozen SUD unions, most of which do not enjoy the same degree of influence.

The failure of reformist politicians to deliver cannot be exposed without making a link between their specific failings over concrete, practical issues and the general question of reformism and its role. Such arguments are obviously more easily won in narrow groupings than in broad confederations. However, simply bypassing the major trade unions offers an organisational substitute for existing structures while leaving the question of how to break the political hold of the bureaucracy over the majority of workers unresolved. In some cases, as the example of the teachers' strike demonstrates, by focusing on general political demands—such as 'Allègre out!'—at the expense of the bread and butter issues of resources which concern all teachers, the *coordinations* proved unable to win over many non-strikers.[50] Some have argued that the *coordinations* represent a return to the syndicalist origins of the French trade union movement,[51] echoing various traditions from the soviets and the International Workers of the World (IWW), and that they reject the disinction between politics and economics.[52] Indeed, the SUD-PTT charter of 1989 explicity identifies with the French syndicalist tradition, evoking the 1906 CGT charter which set out a dual role for the union: the defence of immediate and everyday demands combined with the struggle for the transformation of the whole of society, independent of political parties.[53] But formally rejecting the distinction between politics and economics is not the same as defeating it in practice. Although we can point to many examples of economic struggles feeding political struggles and vice versa over recent years (with the fight against the National Front, discussed below, among the most dramatic), the conflicts opened up since 1995, despite the huge shift in ideas, have yet to go beyond what Marx, in characterising trade union struggle, described as 'a guerilla war against the effects of the existing system',[54] and develop into a generalised attempt to change the system itself. The reproduction of trade union structures, however radical, offers a different set of weapons for waging this guerilla war, but as yet the confidence and solidarity generated by the resurgence of class struggle have yet to crystallise around a political alternative.

Reformism without reforms

A major factor in the Socialist Party's loss of direction during the 1980s was the inability of successive Socialist governments to offer an alternative to the market or the social decay which it left in its wake. During the 1970s the French left had drawn up the 'Common Programme' which pledged to 'smash the domination of big capital' through nationalisations, controls on financial markets and the creation of a national investment bank. François Mitterrand declared that his party would 'rip from the monopolies the instrument of their power by transferring the principal means of production of the private sector to the public sector'.[55] Once elected in 1981 it was Lionel Jospin who put the new government's position in perspective: 'Thus political power is essentially us. Economic power is essentially the dominant sectors of financial and industrial monopoly capitalism. Will there be a clash or a compromise between these two powers?'[56] Since, argued Jospin, the left had chosen to transform the economic system gradually, compromise would be sought.

This 'compromise' saw the Socialists turn on their electorate and wed themselves to an austerity programme, starting in 1983, with devastating results. Despite an increase in gross national product of over a third (the equivalent of a £50 a week increase in the entire population's wages), the proportion of value added (the difference between the overall cost of the manufacturing process and the final value of the product) given over to wages fell from 68.7 percent in 1981 to 60.6 percent in 1993. At the same time, the share given over to investment fell from 20.6 percent in 1970 to 15.4 percent in 1981 and 14.8 percent in 1993. 'What, then, have the companies done with their profits? They have redistributed them to their shareholders (in the form of dividends) and to their creditors (in the form of interest paid to banks or bond holders) or they have invested them on the stockmarket'.[57]

Over the past two decades unemployment has become a fact of life for millions, doubling to around 12 percent of the population. The proportion of France's workforce on very low wages (equivalent to less than half the average wage), has risen to 10 percent, while the average rate of pay has remained virtually unchanged (at around 7,300 francs a month).[58] Those on the minimum wage (around 10 percent of the workforce) have seen their income stagnate and their spending power decline in relation to the average wage since the mid-1980s.[59] The proportion of those in part time work has more than doubled, from 8 percent to 17 percent,[60] and the number of people employed on fixed short term contracts had grown, by 1993, from 9.2 percent to 13.7 percent of the total workforce.[61]

As the need for reforms increased year on year, so the Socialists responded by reining in their ambitions until practically every last vestige of their vision of an alternative society had been relinquished. At its 1987 Lille congress PS values were summarised as follows:

> There is no socialist society in existence today... The socialist movement is therefore more a movement towards socialism, an accumulation of reforms and changes in social relations, a transformation of attitudes and behaviour towards men, than the quest for an end to history... Our task is to pursue this socialist movement, to bring about gradually the birth of a new equilibrium in a composite society, to organise new relations between the individual and the state, between individual freedoms and collective institutions, between private initiative and public intervention.[62]

The dangers of such a limited approach were underlined by a leading

Socialist, Henri Emmanuelli, in 1989:

> *If our party were to renounce its vocation as an instrument of social transformation...to limit itself to managerialism...it would very quickly no longer be a socialist party, but something else altogether... A democratic party perhaps. Or quite simply a dead end.*[63]

By the early 1990s, with the argument that globalisation had narrowed the scope for a voluntaristic role for the state gaining ground within the PS, one set of illusions, the myth of Keynesianism in one country, had effectively been swapped for another, the myth of the impotent nation state. As party secretary, Jospin played an important role in persuading PS activists to accept the retreat from the 1981 programme, declaring in 1987 that 'the period of great reforms' was over.[64] Yet Jospin nevertheless remained, in his own cautious way, an advocate of a greater role for the state. Even at the height of France's liberal turn under the 1986-1988 Chirac government, he remained convinced that the government should actively direct the economy: 'We must say, with more modesty than before, that we are going to take hold of the harness and pull'.[65] When those around him were converted to liberalism Jospin asked, 'When politics are inspired by liberalism, what part do we want our ideas, our socialist instruments to play?'[66] 'The dominant orthodoxy has stifled the debate,' he told *L'Evénement du Jeudi* in 1991.[67] 'Has the time not come to loosen the vice?' When voters emphatically rejected the Socialists' espousal of liberalism in 1993 Jospin declared:

> *The time has come to break with the economic orthodoxy... I want to make it clear that it's not a question of substituting competitive devaluation with competitive deflation, or even to return to 1981. But we must reverse the priorities of our economic policy. Today we set down quantifiable objectives on prices and on the budget deficit, and on unemployment we do what we can. Let's do things the other way round. Let's set quantifiable objectives for jobs and let's see how to meet them!... The dominant model, with which I propose a break— it's not the Socialists who invented it. They rallied to it. This model is not our own, and we would lose our identity in wishing to cling on to it.*[68]

Jospin's election, then, at the head of a Socialist/Communist/Green coalition,[69] appeared to mark a return to old style Keynesian social democratic government, with job creation, the defence of public services and a shorter working week high on its list of priorities. Jospin was keen to distance himself from the overtures to the right that had dominated Mitterrand's second term, and demanded the 'right to an inventory' of his legacy. He cultivated an image of modesty and frankness which stood in direct contrast to the corrupt machinations of Mitterrand and his circle of fawning courtesans. The coalition itself was the fruit of several years of discussion between the Socialists and other left parties which had begun following the 1993 defeat. For the PS the alliance, and Jospin's leadership, represented a return to the values, or at least the rhetoric, of the left.

For the Greens and the PCF, the coalition appeared to offer a route out of marginalisation. The PCF, under the leadership of Robert Hue, is undergoing a period of 'mutation', which involves distancing the organisation from its Stalinist past and recasting it as a mainstream social democratic party, while at the same time claiming to remain a tribune of the oppressed and exploited. This strategy has obviously produced contradictions. The party claims to represent the aspirations of the 'social movement', but it is difficult to see exactly how. For decades the PCF enjoyed a significant influence over the labour movement via its own mass membership, its network of affiliated associations and publications (such as the *Humanité* daily newspaper), its prominent role in local government and the party's domination of the main trade union confederation, the CGT. Until the 1970s the party was the largest in France, both in terms of members and electorate, winning up to a quarter of the vote in parliamentary elections. Now in decline, with its membership falling and its share of the vote consistently below 10 percent, the PCF is gradually relinquishing its hold over the CGT, whose leader, Louis Viannet, resigned from the party's national bureau in December 1996 in order to emphasise the increasing autonomy of the union, although the strong links remain (Viannet was later replaced by railway workers' leader Bernard Thibault, a prominent figure in the December 1995 strikes, as part of the CGT's attempt to rejuvenate its image). *L'Humanité* has now opened up its pages to journalists outside the party and is no longer explicitly identified as the Communist Party newspaper, following an as yet fairly unsuccessful relaunch earlier this year.[70] The party continues to lose support among workers and where new support is emerging it is largely among middle class voters (a poll commissioned by the party in 1997 showed working class support running at 35 percent of the total PCF vote, while support among liberal professionals and managers stood at 36 percent).[71]

In the wake of the left's victory both the PCF and the Greens were at pains to stress the importance of the 'social movement' and their desire to reflect its aspirations in office. 'We in government need strong social movements', declared Green leader Dominique Voynet in January 1998, 'so that we can do our work well and not forget the commitments we made... That's undoubtedly what was missing in 1981 and even more so in 1988, and that explains some of the setbacks and lapses of François Mitterrand's two terms of office'.[72] Following the 1997 election, *The*

New York Times expressed the widespread sense of surprise that a modern industrial power could elect a government on the basis that it would defend working conditions and the welfare state, particularly as Clinton and Blair had given all that up long ago.[73] An editorial in *Le Monde* summed up what was at stake by asking whether the Socialists, 'having won by rehabilitating the idea of a "reformist" party', would be able 'to be really reformist and stand up to the tyranny of the markets'.[74] Those hoping for such a showdown were quickly disappointed. Within days of taking office Jospin had signed up to the Amsterdam stability pact which he himself had denounced only weeks previously as a 'super-Maastricht'. A few weeks later the government stood by as Renault confirmed its proposed closure of the Vilvorde car plant in Belgium, which Jospin himself had demonstrated against the previous March. Despite obtaining a guarantee that alternative employment would be found for the 3,000 strong workforce, the government was hardly standing up to the markets.

The centrepiece of the government's programme is the 35 hour week. The success of the initiative will greatly depend on the second bill, due to be introduced by employment minister Martine Aubry in the autumn of 1999, although the government's decision not to impose a directive from above but to encourage employers and unions to take advantage of the framework provided by the legislation to negotiate their own agreements, and in the process, to revise working practices in their totality, does not bode well for the future. The effectiveness of the legislation has been almost nullified by a concerted offensive by the employers' association, the CNPF (renamed MEDEF in October 1998), whose president, Jean Gandois, referred to the decision to impose a deadline of 1 January 2000 on implementing a 35 hour week[75] as one battle lost in a 'war' which would require a 'killer' to wage. Since he saw his own role as a that of a negotiator he stood down and urged his successor, Ernest Antoine de Seillière, to put up a 'pitiless' fight against the government. De Seillière duly promised to see Jospin off.[76]

So far the employers have come out on top. Of 240 agreements signed by September 1998 only 2,500 jobs had been 'created' (some of them were existing jobs that had been saved). In 75 percent of cases annualisation of working hours (as opposed to calculating them on a monthly basis) was conceded by the unions, while wage levels generally remained unchanged.[77] The principal aim of the legislation, that the 35 hour week would create 700,000 jobs, was a long way from being met. Along with the flexibility created by annualising working hours, the CNPF had reason to congratulate itself on seizing the opportunity opened up by the negotiations. The most glaring case of a negotiated settlement flying in the face of the government's intentions was in the metallurgical industry, where the employers' organisation drew up an agreement with three unions according to which employees would work a maximum ten hour day (12 in exceptional circumstances), a 48 hour week (up from 46 previously), six days a week if necessary with the maximum number of overtime hours raised from 94 to between 180 and 205.[78] As the personnel manager of one major company told *Le Monde*, 'The 35 hours could turn out to be a great opportunity. They give us the chance to rethink the way our work is organised and to negotiate an agreement on wage restraint over several years, which we have never been able to do up to now.' Only one firm in seven, according to one report, intended to take on more workers as a consequence of the legislation, while 64 percent of employers believed the effect on employment generally would be non-existent.[79]

Despite the proposal to end the sale of public companies made in the joint PCF-Socialist Party declaration at the start of the 1997 election campaign, more privatisations have been carried out under the Jospin government than under both the Juppé and Balladur administrations. One of the major privatisations carried out so far, that of Air France, was overseen by the Communist transport minister Jean-Claude Gayssot. 'For as long as I am minister, Air France will not be privatised,' he declared in May 1998, adding, 'The French state will remain a majority shareholder'.[80] Despite Jospin's own hostility to the privatisation of Thomson, Air France and France Télécom in opposition, all, along with the insurance companies GAN and CIC, Société Marseillaise de Crédit, CNP, Aérospatiale and Thomson multimedia, have experienced an 'opening up of capital', the government's preferred term which allowed ministers, such as Gayssot, to deny that putting millions of shares on the market amounted to privatisation. This is despite the fact that the state's share fell, in the case of Air France, from 93 percent to 55 percent, and, in the case of Aérospatiale, below 50 percent.

The employers have not had things all their own way, however. Jospin has constantly been put under pressure by those who elected him. Within six months of taking office his government was jolted by a series of protests and occupations organised by various associations of the unemployed. The growing perception that long term unemployment was a structural problem requiring urgent attention ensured widespread backing for their action. Since 1982 the number of long term unemployed had been multiplied by 2.5, totalling 1,367,000 so that by the end of 1997 two out of five unemployed people were long term unemployed. For around six million people social security payments represent their only source of income. Between 1982 and 1995 the relative level of this income fell below the poverty line, to between 20 percent and 40 percent of average household income.[81] When the government announced a slight rise in social security payments in December 1997 it provoked an outcry from unemployed associations which had been demanding a rise of 1,500 francs a month. The government responded by freeing up funds to head off the protests, but refused to raise payments. Jospin, remarked Ernest-Antoine Seillière, had shown 'true courage', and 'as entrepreneurs, we appreciate this...We cannot fight our battles with one eye on the infirmary'.[82]

Despite eventually agreeing to grant a backdated rise in payments at the end of 1998, the government has so far been unable to quell the protests and remains vulnerable to what one commentator has referred to as 'a latent combativity', ready to break out at the slightest false move on the part of the government.[83] The explosion of anger in French schools in the autumn of 1998, which saw hundreds of thousands of students take to the streets in protest against the scarcity of resources, the occupations of schools by parents and the teachers' strikes of spring 1999, along with numerous other conflicts, such as the lightning transport strike which hit several cities following the death of a Paris Metro worker in June, bear witness to this. So far the government has been able to hold things together. Jospin has astutely stressed his identification with the left, distancing himself from Blair[84] and deliberately provoking ideological clashes with the opposition, accusing the right of being on the wrong side when it came to the abolition of slavery in 1794 and the Dreyfus Affair at the turn of the century, and then calling for the rehabilitation of First World War mutineers.

But the government's hold is fragile and vulnerable to both the left and right. The potential for a right wing backlash was illustrated when government measures that would recognise the legal status of gay couples were defeated by the opposition. With the PS vacillating over whether to go ahead with the legislation, an enormous wave of homophobia was unleashed across Paris in November 1998 in the form of a 100,000 strong demonstration 'in defence of the family'. Meanwhile, the employers' line over the 35 hour week is hardening amid signs that employment minister Martine Aubry will offer them concessions in a new bill on the working week due in the autumn of 1999. Any lingering hopes that the Jospin administration would break with the priorities of its right wing predecessors were dispelled in March 1999 when the NATO bombing campaign began in the Balkans, uniting Jospin and Chirac behind the intervention. The Communist Party strategy of hitching its fortunes to the Socialists muted its opposition to the war, while the decision to open its European election list to various left wing 'personalities', most of whom adopted a hawkish stance from day one and called for the immediate mobilisation of ground troops, further undermined its credibility as a channel for left opposition to Jospin. For the Greens the logic of participation in government was articulated by Daniel Cohn-Bendit, who, having left French politics as a firebrand anti-imperialist icon after May 1968, came back as a pro-NATO apologist for the European single market to lead the Greens' European campaign. In an interview given after the poll he complained that 'in France, there's something that complicates everything; it's the legacy of the strikes of 1995. It's time to go beyond all that'.[85]

Disaffection with mainstream parties is mounting. During the 1980s France's 'parties of government' won around three quarters of the vote in elections. In the late 1990s they were barely able to win half the vote. Polls show that 80 percent of the population believe politicians do not care what they think,[86] while only 26 percent feel represented by a political party.[87] The present period, then, is characterised by a political vacuum, one which, so far, forces to the left of the PS and the Communists have been unable to fill. On the right the events of December 1995 have provoked a crisis which continues to wreak havoc. Chirac's loss of authority, which began with the strikes and was confirmed following his distastrous decision to call an election in 1997, caused the discipline which he had exerted over the right, notably over the question of electoral alliances with the FN (which he opposed), to break down. The simmering debate over what strategy the mainstream right should adopt, given the new mood of the 1990s, resurfaced, this time in the form of a controversy over its relationship with the FN. At the same time, during the regional elections of March 1998, a number of alliances were concluded between the right and the FN, with the result that five members of the UDF, a coalition of various centre right and right wing parties, took the presidency of their respective regional councils with the help of votes from the FN.[88] This marked a new stage in the integration of the FN into the mainstream political spectrum and provoked an outcry, with thousands taking to the streets in protest against the alliances. The UDF coalition was brought to the brink of collapse, with Alain Madelin, leader of Démocratie Libérale (DL), supporting the alliances, and François Bayrou, president of the coalition, opposing them. By May, Madelin and Démocratie Libérale had left the UDF.

The National Front, having caused the break up of France's second largest right wing party after the RPR, was once again at the centre of political life and, at least as far as those who took elections as the principal gauge of a party's strength were concerned, appeared in a virtually unassailable position. A year later, during the European election campaign, the RPR was wracked by divisions of its own. Philippe Séguin, Juppé's successor as RPR leader and head of the party's election slate, caused a sensation when he resigned only weeks before the poll, claiming that Chirac and his supporters were undermining him. Chirac was forced to turn to Nicolas Sarkozy, a man who had been jeered by the RPR congress only four years previously for supporting Balladur's 1995 presidential bid. Sarkozy assumed temporary control of the party and fronted the election campaign alongside Alain Madelin. Immediately after the election Sarkozy resigned, having polled only 12.7 percent of the vote, trailing the slate put up by Philippe de Villiers, a maverick nationalist aristocrat, and Charles Pasqua, a founder member of the RPR from the right of the party, who scored 13 percent. Pasqua claimed, in the wake of Chirac's backing for the NATO intervention in the Balkans and given his support for greater European integration, to represent a return to true Gaullist values of national independence and grandeur. To this end he announced that he was forming a new party with de Villiers, the Rassemblement pour la France. By this time, however, the FN was no longer in a position to dominate the recomposition of the right, having itself split in December 1998, only months after its triumph in the regional poll the previous March.

The National Front in crisis

The impetus given to the anti-racist movement by the events of December 1995 has had a devastating effect on the fortunes of the FN and its leader, Jean-Marie Le Pen, the hitherto unassailable figurehead of the French far right, who was forced to look on helplessly as his organisation began tearing itself apart. One of the most enjoyable spectacles of 1998 was the sight of Le Pen in December, his authority seriously under threat, condemning those who had dared to challenge him as extremists, racists and fascists, who, he claimed, were using Trotskyist tactics to undermine him as part of a plot jointly financed by the president, US imperialism and international freemasonry. The split has largely been portrayed as one based on personal rivalry between Le Pen and Bruno Mégret. Although this is an important element of the conflict it reflects a much deeper crisis of the extreme right. The defensive position in which the Front has been placed as a result of the strikes and the revival of a militant anti-racist movement has caused the diverse elements that make it up to pull in different directions. The Front has experienced a crisis of the leadership cult which enabled it to federate the entire extreme right. This means that not only has the illusion of Le Pen as an omnipotent force guiding the Front been tainted but the federative strategy which held the organisation together has hit the buffers. After briefly outlining the strategy developed by Le Pen over the past three decades, this section examines how the FN's strategy has been knocked off course by the new mood.

The FN strategy: For 15 years the Front enjoyed almost unremitting success in embedding itself in national and local political life. The strategy developed by its founders in the early 1970s was to cultivate an image of respectability in order to reach out beyond its own narrow ranks and then set about transforming this new audience 'in our image'.[89] This was based on the analysis that the stabilisation of capitalism during the post-war economic boom, along with the decline of the traditional petty bourgeoisie and the creation of a layer of civil servants loyal to the state bureaucracy, had, along with the experience of the Second World War and the Holocaust, fundamentally altered the conditions in which fascists were operating. This meant that the road to power would be a long haul and would have to combine a strategy of legitimisation, of apparent allegiance to the rules of liberal democracy, with an attempt to build an extra-parliamentary base.[90]

One of Le Pen's major achievements was to pay lip service to the rules of the parliamentary game while pursuing a strategy of radicalisation. He ruthlessly ensured that the Front remained both within and without the established party set-up, constantly risking defections by obliging his followers to defend the most extreme positions, from Holocaust denial to racial supremacy. At the same time he ensured the cohesiveness of the organisation by demanding first of all absolute allegiance to the Front's hierarchy of leaders and secondly by housing the different factions that made up the organisation in a system of parallel internal structures. This strategy had two advantages. Firstly, the leading lights of the various currents that had rallied to the FN could be given positions of responsibility. Secondly, by pitting them against each other, rivals to Le Pen's succession could be neutralised. In the 1970s the influence of François Duprat, to all intents and purposes Le Pen's deputy, was held in check by the national secretary, Victor Barthélemy. In the 1980s Le Pen's main rival, Jean-Pierre Stirbois, had his influence as national secretary curtailed by the creation of the post of chairman filled by Bruno Mégret. In the 1990s Mégret's increasing predominance was countered by the creation of a rival power base when Le Pen appointed Bruno Gollnisch to the beefed up post of national secretary.

For the past 20 years, success both in terms of votes and recruitment bound the organisation around the personality of Le Pen. At FN central committee meetings monarchists and fundamentalist Catholics sat alongside Pagans and veterans of the Waffen SS, while mercenaries,[91] ex-collaborators and former leaders of right wing terrorist opposition to French withdrawal from Algeria brushed shoulders with Moonies, company directors and former Gaullists. Le Pen embodied the contradictory nature of the Front: a millionaire who proclaimed himself a 'man of the people'; a divorcee thrown out of a church for

urinating in the font when a student, yet idolised by the party's reactionary Catholic wing; publicly hailed as a 'man of destiny'[92] by those
who were later to plot his overthrow; and promoted in the mid-1980s
as the 'French Reagan' by those who now applaud his protectionist
opposition to globalisation.

The FN on the defensive: Within six months of celebrating its 15 percent
score in the parliamentary elections of June 1997, the illusion of the Front
as an invincible monolith was to be blown apart. Events since December
1995 had thrown the organisation off course. During the strike wave the
emptiness of the FN's claims to represent ordinary workers had been
increasingly evident. The strikes, characterised by Le Pen as a 'revolt of
the privileged', were denounced by the party leadership as 'archaic and
ruinous'. But opinion polls showed that 71 percent of the Front's electorate supported them.[93] The surge of anti-racist activity further
marginalised the FN. The series of protests in support of the *sans-papiers*
and the mobilisations against the anti-immigrant legislation proposed by
Jean-Louis Debré marked a sea change in attitudes to the immigration
issue. For the first time in over a decade those who opposed the scapegoating of immigrants found themselves on the offensive. Everywhere
FN leaders went they found crowds of demonstrators ready to oppose
them.

Aware that December 1995 had radically altered the political climate,
the Front was forced to respond to the changing situation or face
becoming irrelevant. Its response was to pursue the dual strategy that had
proved so successful in the past. This involved on the one hand acting as
a pole of attraction for the weakest elements of the traditional right,
entering into electoral alliances with them where possible, and on the
other bolstering its status as an anti-establishment party by reinforcing its
network of extra-parliamentary satellite organisations. But the polarisation of French society now worked against the FN. The electoral defeat
of the right had weakened the cohesion which Chirac's dominance had
provided, opening up the possibility that sections of the right would
depart from his strategy of refusing electoral alliances with the FN. But
at the very moment when the attraction of alliances was growing, opposition to the FN, which was already hindering its attempts to infiltrate the
workplace, drew out the hardline elements at the FN's core which in turn
endangered the image of respectability essential for the conclusion of
electoral alliances with the mainstream right. The Front's room for
manoeuvre was further inhibited by an internal crisis which was to see
Le Pen's strategy unravel before his eyes.

Crisis of legitimacy: Put on the defensive, the culture of brutality at the heart of the FN was forced out into the open. In October 1996 an anti-racist demonstration in Monceau-les-Mines was attacked by an armed and helmeted branch of the Front's security force, a 'secret' unit of former marines, one of whom boasted to the press that they were capable of overthrowing a government within 48 hours.[94] At the Strasbourg congress in March 1997, while 50,000 marched outside, the Front chose to present its legal face, revising its constitution and proclaiming its fidelity to the 'institutions of the Republic and democratic pluralism'.[95] But outside the hall, the organisation's security force presented a different face, several of them getting arrested for impersonating riot police and carrying out bogus identity checks on the demonstrators. During the truckers' strike of 1997 FN members in Mégret-run Vitrolles, led by the head of the municipal police force, attacked a picket line, seriously injuring a striker.[96]

For over a decade both Mégret and Le Pen had been united on the need for the Front to avoid becoming a part of the established party system and on the value of tactical electoral alliances with the traditional right. In two important ways the situation had now changed. Firstly, the crisis that had put the FN on the backfoot was also damaging the traditional right. The Front, and Mégret in particular, saw an opportunity to profit from the disarray of these disoriented and directionless parties by making tactical alliances with them. The alliance with Charles Millon in the Rhône-Alpes region in March 1998, concluded by Gollnisch, bore witness to this. Secondly, however, Mégret had gradually established his dominance over the party apparatus, coming top of the central committee elections at the 1997 congress, and positioning himself as the natural successor to the 70 year old Le Pen. This was a serious setback for those in the party, in particular the old guard of the French extreme right (fundamentalist Catholics, veterans of Vichy and Algeria, founder members of the FN), Le Pen included, who acknowledged Mégret's uses but despised him as an arriviste technocrat.[97]

With the FN in a defensive position these differences were magnified, with rival factions blaming each other for every setback and seeking opportunities to undermine one another. Internal rivalry became an obstacle to escaping the rut the FN found itself in. This is particularly evident in the organisation's attempt, led by Mégret, to strengthen its base in the workplace and in working class areas. Mégret himself took to leafleting workers at factory gates, turning up outside a Moulinex plant threatened with closure in Sarthe, in the Loire, in October 1996 and leafleting France Télécom workers threatened with privatisation the following September. He also set up an FN trade union for Paris Metro workers and ensured that the Front stood candidates for election to council housing committees. These efforts were hampered by Mégret's opponents, notably Bruno Gollnisch, who set up his own transport union in Lyon, and Le Pen's son in law Samuel Maréchal, who set up the National Circle of Unionised Workers to group together FN members in the unions.

Maréchal, deputy to Gollnisch, also runs the Front's youth wing, the Front National de la Jeunesse (FNJ), an organisation rivalled by the pro-Mégret student organisation, the Renouveau Etudiant (RE). Following the victory of Mégret's supporters in elections to the FN central committee in March 1997, Le Pen allowed Jean-Claude Martinez to set up yet another counterweight to Mégret's influence, in the form of a shadow cabinet. Mégret, in turn, formed his own security force to prevent the FN's official security unit from keeping track of his movements. Le Pen's strategy of creating parallel structures to house rival factions was now spiralling out of control.

Crisis of leadership: In describing the cult of leadership developed around Hitler by the Nazis, Trotsky drew a parallel with the fate of Alfonso XIII of Spain, forced to flee the country when the Republic was declared in 1931:

> *Naive minds think that the office of kingship lodges in the king himself, in his ermine cloak and his crown, in his flesh and bones. As a matter of fact, the office of kingship is an interrelation between people. The king is king only because the interests and prejudices of millions of people are refracted through his person. When the flood of development sweeps away these interrelations, then the king appears to be only a washed-out man with a flabby lower lip.*[98]

The mutual exchange of recriminations among FN factions were beginning to damage the cult of leadership which had defined the organisation for 25 years. Already Mégret's success in winning the town of Vitrolles in 1997 had convinced Le Pen not to stand as a candidate in either the parliamentary or local elections later that year for fear of being overshadowed by Mégret. For the first time since 1981 the Front went into a national election without its leader as a candidate. His prestige damaged, Le Pen was then successfully opposed by the FN *bureau politique* on two occasions, firstly between the two rounds of the 1997 election when both Mégret and Gollnisch publicly distanced themselves from his stated preference for a Socialist majority, and again in March 1998 when Le Pen demanded that the endorsement of the principle of national preference (priority rights for French nationals over immigrants) be made a condition of electoral alliances with other right wing parties.[99] Le Pen's ability to continue as FN president was now openly questioned in the press,[100] forcing him to assert his leadership by differentiating himself from Mégret.

Le Pen drew attention to the different conclusions each had reached concerning the position in which they had been placed post-1995. As far as he was concerned, the crisis of French society ran so deep that the FN was unlikely to remain trapped in a defensive position indefinitely. The Front must at all costs retain its status as an outsider in order to benefit from the bankruptcy of the mainstream parties. The Front should therefore 'embody the alternative to the system', claimed Maréchal, while another Le Pen loyalist, Carl Lang, attempted to undermine Mégret by invoking a maxim attributed to Lenin, 'Unity at the top, never! Unity at the base, always!'[101] The Front's failure to advance beyond a 15 percent share of the vote, or translate electoral success into members, however, was a source of frustration. Much of the party cadre believed the organisation would advance more quickly if it followed Mégret's strategy of electoral alliances with the right which, he argued, would allow the FN to play a dominant role in the restructuring of the party system. His arm had been strengthened by the attitude of several leading figures on the right. One of de Gaulle's most faithful acolytes, Alain Peyrefitte, concluded in the wake of the right's election defeat that alliances with the FN should be considered, although not while Le Pen remained leader.[102] The case for alliances with the FN was also put by two of France's leading bosses, Ambroise Roux[103] and Jacques Calvet,[104] while former Gaullist prime minister Edouard Balladur proposed setting up a commission, open to the far right, which would publicly debate the FN's ideas on 'national preference'.[105] Responding to claims that alliances would soften the Front's image Mégret replied:

> The strategy I am putting forward has nothing to do with Gianfranco Fini's in Italy, who had renounced his programme and turned his movement into something totally bland so that it may gain acceptance from the establishment. I who have put into action the policy of national preference in Vitrolles...will never accept that the movement compromises itself and abandons any aspect of its values or programme.[106]

Le Pen and his followers were not opposed to electoral agreements but they did not see them as the Front's priority. If the goal of such alliances was to ensure the return of proportional representation, argued Le Pen, giving the FN 60 deputies and five ministers, 'it's totally useless. I'd even say it would be harmful. That would kill the only hope the French have left'.[107]

Although these differences arose from a genuine divergence over what strategy to adopt, they had the advantage of allowing Le Pen to expose what many saw as Mégret's principal weakness, his distant manner and effete technocratic style. In contrast to his own rough and ready populist image, Mégret lacked, according to Le Pen, 'popular fibre'.[108] So when Mégret openly advocated alliances in the aftermath of the 1997 election, Le Pen deliberately tried to scupper the initiative (not least because sections of the traditional right were only prepared to contemplate such a move under Mégret's leadership), and to stress both the Front's anti-establishment status and his own street fighting credentials. It was in this context that Le Pen's attack on the Socialist candidate in Mantes-la-Jolie between the two rounds of the 1997 election took place, during the course of which he pinned her against a wall and tried to rip the Republican sash from around her body, scratching and insulting her until his own bodyguards pulled him away. Six months later, at a joint press conference in Munich alongside the former Waffen SS officer and Republikaner Party leader Franz Schönhuber, Le Pen declared that the Germans 'were the martyred people of Europe' and went on to reiterate his belief that the Holocaust was a minor detail of the Second World War.[109]

When things finally came to a head towards the end of 1998, Le Pen acted decisively, knowing that his status as a leader figure depended on maintaining the illusion that he was the all-powerful presence driving the FN forward. In November he informed staff at the party headquarters that only his portrait could appear on its walls.[110] Having denied Mégret the right to head the Front's European election list by nominating his wife,[111] thus avoiding the possibility of a Mégret bandwagon threatening his own chances of being the Front's candidate for the 2002 presidential election, Le Pen then expelled two Mégret supporters for having circulated an internal document critical of him.

Mégret, in turn, made his appeal to the party on the grounds that Le Pen's leadership was incapable of building a party of government. It had become 'bunkerised', with Le Pen 'contested', 'isolated' and surrounded by courtesans, wasting party funds on parallel structures designed to reduce Mégret's influence. But the criticisms made of Le Pen and his cronies were not simply about personal rivalry, they reflected frustration within the FN at its threefold crisis: its activist base was diminishing, its satellite organisations were little more than empty shells, and the party cadre was weak and inexperienced. Several leading Le Pen allies were singled out by the Mégretists as barriers to growth. All were criticised for their personal failure to retain members and build effective federations. The final straw was Le Pen's nomination of his rich wife to head the European campaign, a woman whose 'temperament, attitude, standard of living, all added up to a bourgeois candidate cut off from our most popular electorate'.[112]

Neither Mégret nor Le Pen did particularly well in the European elections: Le Pen had to contend with rumblings of discontent within his party after polling only 5.69 percent, and Mégret, having scored 3.28 percent and with his Mouvement National in severe financial straits, had to apply for readmission into the public service post he had left when he went into politics. The scores of the respective formations were not the only indication of the extent to which the extreme right had lost ground. In 1995 pollsters had attributed to the FN 27 percent of working class votes in the presidential election. By 1999 this figure had fallen to 6 percent. Immigration, for so long at the heart of political debate, came last in the list of voter preoccupations, with 22 percent citing it as a major factor in their choice of candidate, against 65 percent for unemployment and 45 percent for the defence of social reforms.[113] Various polls have shown that Mégret has the support of more party functionaries than Le Pen, and that Le Pen has more support among FN voters. History has shown that it is possible for more than one fascist organisation to coexist in France; in the 1930s the Croix de Feu and Jaques Doriot's Parti Populaire Français both mobilised tens of thousands of supporters. The present situation has seriously damaged the the extreme right, but its electorate will not simply disappear overnight. It is also possible that Le Pen's party could emerge hardened and more cohesive from the split.[114] Above all, however, the past few years have demonstrated that when the extreme right is consistently put on the defensive it finds it much harder to grow.

The struggle continues

The scale of the crisis of French society and the hopes for change engendered by the December strikes have ensured that the issues they raised have not faded. Above all, nobody involved could forget what had happened:

> The general impression was of a melting pot...of discontentment faced with the unbearable concrete conditions of work, or the unbearable conditions of life. Unbearable, not in a technocratic or economistic sense, but unbearable from the point of view of human existence in a socially concrete form: workstations, pay slips, salary deductions, the extra years of work, the fear of unemployment...[115]

France in the 1990s has seen a tremendous backlash against the liberal economic orthodoxy of the 1980s, witnessed in the remarkable sales of books critical of the free market, such as Pierre Bourdieu's *La Misère du Monde* and Viviane Forreser's *L'Horreur Economique*; in the revival of the monthly *Le Monde Diplomatique*, which, having become a forum for analysis and debate on the left, now sells 200,000 copies in France alone; and in the return of class as a subject for French cinema.[116] Another manifestation of the shift to the left has been the electoral success of the socialist organisation Lutte Ouvrière (LO), whose candidate, Arlette Laguiller, won 1.6 million votes in the 1995 presidential poll and achieved a similar score in the general election of 1997. The joint socialist slate put up by LO/Ligue Communiste Révolutionnaire (LCR) for the 1999 European elections performed impressively, scoring over 5 percent of the vote and sending the first Trotskyist deputies to the European parliament.

All of the above examples reflect, in different ways, the thirst for an alternative to the misery which the market inflicts on people's lives. So far this has not, as we have seen, translated into the emergence of a credible political alternative to the plural left. As Trotsky argued in the 1930s:

> *Politics may be defined as the art of taking advantage of favourable situations. In France, at present, you have an exceptional situation, full of opportunities. It is necessary to know how to take advantage of it. That means not to try to stay in this calm bay, but to take to the open sea.*[117]

Yet both the two main organisations of the revolutionary left have experienced problems in taking to the open sea. One obvious question concerns Lutte Ouvrière. Despite its remarkable success in contesting elections on a platform proposing wage rises, job creation programmes and nationalisations, the organisation itself has not grown significantly since 1995. Why? One explanation is that LO has simply misjudged the current mood. It does not believe its own electoral success to be indicative of any kind of radicalisation on the part of French workers.[118] Indeed, during the month of December 1995 Arlette Laguiller publicly bemoaned the 'demoralisation and apoliticisation' of the working class.[119] The 1995 strikes, and those that followed in their wake, were interpreted as struggles driven and controlled by the bureaucracies of the main trade union confederations rather than the rank and file, leading LO to conclude:

> *The possibilities for revolutionary activists to play a leading role, outflanking these organisations in line with the basic interests of workers in significant movements, are reduced. Reduced does not mean that we should not strive to ensure that all struggles go as far as they can, or further [sic], because we cannot neglect the effect on consciousness of the struggles themselves, but we must not cultivate ultra-left illusions about current*

possibilities by overestimating the importance of the recent movements.[120]

Moreover, the organisation's leadership argued, Lutte Ouvrière should have no illusions about its own ability to convince workers to take up the demands contained in its 'Emergency plan for workers' ('Plan d'urgence pour les travailleurs'), or about their capacity to apply any of the measures, begging the question, if LO could not take its plan seriously, why should anyone else?[121]

While Laguiller has become a nationally known figure, LO has failed to go beyond the abstract propagandism which has brought such electoral success and to take advantage of, or even recognise, the fact that the tide of events has been flowing in its favour. Along with its narrow and pessimistic analysis of economic struggles, the organisation's most serious failing has been its failure to mobilise around key political issues. This has been most apparent with regard to the rise of the National Front. Since the emergence of the FN as a major political player in the mid-1980s LO has made no attempt to build a united front against the threat, arguing that a revival in class struggle will sweep it away:

> *It is vital for the future of the working class that the ideas of the FN in the workplace are beaten back. But this can only be done on the basis of a revival of the ideas and attitudes of class struggle, which would give workers a real perspective of struggle against job insecurity, unemployment, and low wages. This kind of revival of the labour movement is the only means of effectively confronting the FN and its false radicalism, based on reactionary ideas and an anti-worker programme.*[122]

This outlook partly explains LO's dismissive attitude towards anti-FN mobilisations. The February 1996 demonstration against the racist Debré laws, for example, the biggest and angriest demonstration against anti-immigrant legislation in a decade, was not only ignored by LO but the film makers who organised it were publicly condemned by the organisation for being cut off 'from the preoccupations of workers, including the vast majority of immigrant workers'.[123] The 50,000 strong protest in 1997 against the FN congress in Strasbourg was dismissed by LO as 'festive', 'folklorique', and 'apolitical, not to say anti-political':

> *It would require great naivety to believe that a march, even a big one, whether joyous like the one at Strasbourg or solemn, or that a picnic a few hundred metres from the place where the FN was holding its conference, might hinder the growth of its influence.*[124]

Leaving aside for a moment the fact that, as we have seen, such protests did precisely this, what is LO's principal objection to such marches? Given the Socialist and Communist participation in many of the demonstrations,[125] LO deduced that 'to say that these demonstrations are better than nothing is to make out that if the left was back in government in a year, then the conditions for fighting the National Front would become more favourable'.[126] Such attitudes are not merely sectarian, they amount to an abstention on the question of fighting fascism and a cavalier disregard for the way in which racism has been systematically used by all parties in the context of, and often as a direct result of, the rise of the FN, dividing workers and hindering their ability to fight back. This was brought out in the wake of the March 1998 demonstration mentioned at the beginning of this article, which LO shunned on the grounds that the targets of the march were the right wing politicians who had concluded electoral agreements with the FN, rather than the Front itself, implying that the demonstration served the interests not just of the Socialists, but also of those on the right who had not made alliances with the FN:

> *...even without the physical participation of the right, a Republican front atmosphere hung around the demonstration. In any case it conveyed the illusion that the fight against Le Pen is based on the unity of all those who proclaim republican values.*[127]

Responding to criticism from the Ligue Communiste Révolutionnaire (LCR) that LO had betrayed its Trotskyist roots in disavowing its own call to attend the march only a few days beforehand,[128] LO accused those who participated in the demonstration of giving 'their backing to political forces which bear a crushing responsibility in the rise of the FN'.[129]

This was nonsense. The demonstration, organised by a collective of left wing parties, anti-racist associations and trade unions, was not only militantly anti-FN but fiercely critical of other parties, not least the Socialists, who were berated throughout by a contingent of teachers from Seine-Saint-Denis (who themselves had been attacked prior to the march by the Socialist education minister Claude Allègre who argued their strike was 'playing the FN's game'). Moreover, the resignation of those who had allied with the FN would have damaged first and foremost the Front and dealt a severe blow to its quest for legitimacy.

One of the reasons for the inadequacy of LO's analysis of the situation derives from its weak theoretical grasp of fascism:

> *The Front National represents a more radical policy for the right. For the moment, more in the area of verbal demagogy than in reality. But this verbal radicalism may turn into a violent, anti-worker radicalism if the bosses arrive at the conviciton that, to maintain or increase their profits, it is necessary to smash the working class and if it makes this conviction concrete by financing*

the extreme right.[130]

While in an abstract sense there is little to disagree with here, one crucial element is missing from the explanation. In order to prove itself worthy of financial backing the fascist party must build an organisation which looks capable of leading an onslaught on the labour movement. A fundamental stage in the rise of fascism is therefore the autonomous development of its party, which, as we have seen, is based on both the quest for legitimacy and the construction of an extra-parliamentary base.[131] Part of the ABC of anti-fascism is therefore to hinder this autonomous development, both by exposing the fascist party's anti-democratic aims and by disrupting its efforts to ingratiate itself into the political mainstream, the latter being particularly important for fascist organisations in the post-war period.[132]

While LO's abstention from serious, consistent anti-fascist activity is based in part on a failure to come to terms with the aims and tactics adopted by the FN, it also forms part of a deliberate strategy to focus almost exclusively on building in the workplace,[133] hence the relatively low profile of LO in movements such as those of the *sans-papiers* and the unemployed of the mid to late 1990s, characterised by the organisation as 'worthy' but ultimately 'marginal in relation to the labour movement'.[134] LO's self-limiting and one-dimensional outlook undoubtedly contributed to the inability of anti-fascist groups during the 1980s and early 1990s to go beyond sporadic and inconsistent opposition to the FN. More recently, however, LO's pessimism has affected its ability to grasp the opportunities offered by the current climate and seriously undermined the possibility of forging links between those who take action over political issues, such as racist legislation, and those who are involved in industrial struggle.

Like LO, the LCR has experienced problems in trying to adapt to the new mood. The LCR has had a much greater presence than LO in the various associations which have sprung up since 1995, winning respect for the role which its members have played as leading activists in a range of bodies, from the breakaway SUD unions, the AC! unemployed groups, the CADAC association for a woman's right to choose, or the anti-FN organisation Ras l'Front. Indeed, its members are often known more for their role in such bodies than for their activities as members of the LCR. The criticism that neither LO or the Ligue use their newspapers as an organising tool has already been made in this journal and remains valid.[135] For the LCR, this, along with its practice of expending its energies in the creation of countless breakaway groups and associations, is symptomatic of a tendency to seek short cuts on the road to building a party. Despite the dynamism and commitment of LCR members involved in a whole range of activities, unless concrete action around specific issues is related not just to wider political questions but to an alternative vision of how society could be organised any attempt to forge a genuine political challenge to the mainstream left will remain a pipe dream. At present the Ligue refers to the need to 'bring about a break on the left with liberalism using mobilisations seeking to impose aspirations partially taken up by the plural left during its electoral campaign and which remain for the most part unsatisfied today'.[136] At a time when the audience for revolutionary ideas is growing, the Ligue offers little in the way of leadership beyond vague slogans about the need to create a 'left of the left' and appears distracted by the desire to be part of a realignment of socialists and communists into a broad left grouping.

In the 1930s Trotsky warned of the consequences for those who vacillated over the question of the independence of the revolutionary party:

Whatever may be the social sources and political causes of opportunistic mistakes and deviations, they are always reduced ideologically to an erroneous understanding of the revolutionary party, of its relation to other proletarian organisations and to the class as a whole... One of the psychological sources of opportunism is a superficial impatience, a lack of confidence in the gradual growth of the party's influence, the desire to win the masses by organisational manoeuvres or personal diplomacy. Out of this springs the policy of combinations behind the scenes, the policy of silence, of hushing up, of self-renunciation, of adaptation to the ideas and slogans of others; and finally, the complete passage to the positions of opportunism.[137]

Although such criticism may seem harsh when applied to the LCR, it loses none of its relevance in the light of the French left's failure to build any effective opposition to the NATO bombing of Yugoslavia. Aside from the two demonstrations (on 23 March and 1 April 1999) called as an immediate response to the NATO intervention, no further mobilisations, no network of anti-war committees, no teach-ins or meetings or rallies on the question of the war were organised during the entire ten week bombing campaign. Yet during the three weeks prior to the European election the Ligue alone organised over 50 public campaign meetings, including joint meetings with LO in 15 cities across France. Having made the decision to direct their energies and resources into running an election campaign rather than an anti-war campaign, did the two organisations transform their meetings into anti-war rallies and use them as a springboard for anti-war activity? Not a single word of the extracts reprinted in *Lutte Ouvrière* of Arlette Laguiller's speech delivered to thousands of socialists at the LO fête in May referred to the war, nor was it mentioned on a single leaflet for the Paris election rally on 6 June, during the course of which neither Alain Krivine, LCR spokesperson, nor Laguiller, chose to put the war at the centre of their speeches to the 5,000 present.

Why did the two main organisations of the far left in France fail the test of the war so abjectly? The war exposed, in fairly dramatic fashion, some of the weaknesses referred to above, notably Lutte Ouvrière's essentially passive approach to political mobilisations and the LCR's lack of political clarity. 'It is particularly difficult to speak out (not to mention to mobilise) against Greater Serbian nationalism and at the same time NATO's intervention in this crisis,' declared the LCR newspaper *Rouge* at the start of the war, adding, 'However, it must be done'.[138] But the even-handedness of the Ligue's coverage of the war, which put US imperialism on an equal footing with the Milosevic regime, blunted its ability to offer a decisive lead and led it to criticise others who opposed the war, from those who took part in the magnificent anti-war demonstrations in Greece to the intellectual Régis Debray, for lending support to Milosevic.[139] LO's coverage, while clear and decisive in the abstract, meant very little in concrete, practical terms. The irony of the situation is that the the war highlighted, infinitely more than the various anti-fascist and anti-racist demonstrations attended by Socialist politicians, the hypocrisy of the Jospin government which used the rhetoric of humanitarianism to lend support to the brutal imposition of NATO power in the Balkans. Here was the opportunity to draw a line in the sand between the government and the rest of the left and build an effective opposition to its policies home and abroad and in the process lay the basis for a clear and uncompromising political alternative. Compared with such a prospect 5 percent of the European election poll and a handful of MEPs must now seem a meagre consolation.

Conclusion

The 1990s in France have been characterised by polarisation and volatility. This article has argued that the tide has turned away from the right in recent years. Despite Jospin's ability to dampen the groundswell of anger at large in French society the present period is still characterised by the 'latent combativity' that we have referred to here. But the revival of fortunes of the Socialists themselves speaks volumes about the capacity of apparently moribund political formations to regenerate themselves. This does not just apply to social democracy. If a tide taken on the flood leads on to fortune, France's history is littered with examples of the opposite happening when powerful surges to the left have been succeeded by a reactionary backlash. The Paris Commune of 1871 was drowned in blood, the Popular Front of 1936-1938 gave way to Vichy, and the events of May 1968 were followed in June by a right wing election victory. More recently the Mitterrand victory of 1981 was followed by the emergence of the National Front. Jospin's government has so far managed to tread a fine line between the hopes engendered by December 1995 and the demands of the employers. There is evidence to suggest that the employers' line is hardening. The outcome of this stand-off will depend in part on the ability of those on the left to offer an alternative to Jospin's illusory vision of a 'market economy without a market society'.

One of the constant refrains of Europe's newly elected social democratic governments has been the need to ensure wealth creation before distribution. Such claims fly in the face of the reality of production under capitalism. Between 1969 and 1994 global production rose from $360 to $4,500 per head. During that time the poorest third of the world's population has seen its share of global resources fall from 2.3 percent to 1.1 percent, while the share of the richest fifth has risen from 69 percent to 86 percent. In a world where a third of people living in developing countries have no drinking water, where over a third of all children suffer malnutrition and where the director of the Disney corporation can earn $203 million in a single year,[140] the need for an alternative to the anarchy of capitalist society is clear. In France, as we have seen, events of the past few years have led increasing numbers to seek an alternative. The chasm that divides political parties from society is widening. At the same time, the strikes and protests described here underline that after years of resignation and defeat French workers are rediscovering their combativity. This creates a situation of tremendous volatility. In such conditions, as we have seen, the audience for revolutionary ideas grows, offering opportunities even for the smallest of organisations, 'on the proviso that this small party discerns in its smallness not an advantage but the greatest misfortune of which it must be rid as speedily as possible'.[141]

Notes

1   I am very grateful to Ian Birchall, Sebastian Budgen, Denis Godard and Paul McGarr for reading and commenting on the draft of this article.
2   TF1 evening news, 21 January 1998.
3   In January 1996 Marseilles tram workers won hands down on the question of maintaining a single status for all workers and struck again the following March against the annualisation of working hours. In Toulouse tram workers struck in December of the same year and won a 35 hour week with no loss of pay.
4   TF1 evening news, 21 January 1998.
5   *Libération*, 16 December 1998. Cintegabelle is Jospin's constituency.
6   J G Shields, 'Immigration Politics in Mitterrand's France', in G Raymond (ed), *France During the Socialist Years* (Aldershot, 1994).
7   For an account of the events of November-December 1995, see C Harman, 'France's Hot December', *International Socialism* 70 (Spring 1996). Among the most useful studies in French are S Béroud and R Mouriaux (eds), *Le souffle de décembre. Le mouvement de décembre 1995. Continuitiés, singularités, portée* (Paris, 1997); S Béroud, R Mouriaux and M Vakaloudis, *Le mouvement social en*

France. Essai de sociologie politique (Paris, 1998); C Leneveu and M Vakaloulis, *Faire mouvement. Novembre-décembre 1995* (Paris, 1998).

8   On 13 October over 200,000 demonstrated across France, including 16,000 in Toulouse, almost the entire school student population of the city. On 15 October half a million demonstrated in 350 towns and, on 20 October, 300,000.

9   Cited in J Jackson, 'De Gaulle and May 1968', in H Gough and J Horne (eds), *De Gaulle and Twentieth Century France* (London, 1994).

10   J-M Colombani, *Le Résident de la République* (Paris, 1998).

11   See P Fysh, 'Gaullism and the Liberal Challenge', unpublished PhD thesis (University of London, 1990).

12   P Reinhard, *Chronique d'un naufrage programmé: La fin de la Cinquième République* (Paris, 1998), p69. For Chirac, one of his friends commented, 'ideas are gadgets; their only use is to win elections' (ibid, p94).

13   The differences between the two men were plain to see when each visited the annual Salon de l'Agriculture in Paris. Chirac was happy to pass the day roaming from stand to stand discussing the relationship between the weight of a bull and the size of its testicles. The hapless Balladur was ill at ease and asked all the wrong questions. See *Le Monde*, 21 April 1995.

14   'I didn't vote for him', recalled a Paris Metro worker, 'but there was something about the campaign, it put a smile back on our faces', *Le Monde*, 5 December 1995.

15   C Harman, op cit, pp61-62.

16   V Maurus, 'Il faut y aller plein pot!', *Le Monde*, 30 November 1995.

17   Ibid.

18   The paper was *Infomatin* which later folded, though the two events are not connected.

19   *Le Monde*, 5 December 1995.

20   N Béniès, 'Réformes, changement et mouvement social', *Utopie Critique* 8 (1996).

21   'Pour une réforme de la Sécurité Sociale', *Le Monde*, 3-4 December 1995.

22   *Le Monde*, 20 December 1995.

23   J Fitoussi and P Rosanvallon, *Le nouvel âge des inégalités* (Paris, 1996), p62.

24   D Berger, 'A la recherche du mouvement social', *Futur antérieur* 35/36 (1996), p8.

25   S Béroud et al (eds), op cit, p106.

26   Citied in P Cours-Salies, 'Un espoir en partie formulé', in C Leneveu and M Vakalouis (eds), op cit, pp244-245.

27   *Le Monde*, 10 February 1994. Cited in S Béroud et al (eds), op cit, p19.

28   M Noblecourt, 'L'ébranlement du syndicalisme français', *Etudes* (September 1996), p181.

29   J-M Pernot, 'Les syndicats à l'epreuve de l'actualité', *Regards sur l'actualité* (June 1996), p12.

30   S Béroud et al (eds), op cit, p20.

31   Cited in M Kail, 'Tous ensemble. Une grève se gère par les grévistes', *Les Temps Modernes* 587 (March/April 1996), p459.

32   Cited in S Béroud and J Capdevielle, 'En finir avec une approche culpabilisée et culpabilisante du corporatisme', in C Leneveu and M Vakaloulis, op cit, pp96-97.

33   Cited in M Kail, op cit, p459.

34   'What happened at the start of the week is what many of us have been fighting to bring about for years: there is no more sectionalism on the part of the drivers, and it came about naturally, as if by magic. The worst thing is that we're surprised by it, because it ought to go without saying' (CFDT activist cited in P Barets, 'Journal de grève. Notes de terrain', *Actes de la recherche en sciences sociales* 115 (1996), p12.

35   Ibid.

36   I Birchall, *Bailing Out the System: Reformist Socialism in Western Europe 1945-1985* (London, 1986), p124.

37   A Bertho, 'La grève dans tous ses états', *Futur antérieur* 33/34 (1996), p67.

38   J Pons, 'La chance perdue des syndicats', *Les Temps Modernes* 586, January-February 1996, p32.

39   Interview with CGT railway workers' leader Bernad Thibault, *Futur antérieur* 33/34 (1996), p50.

40   Cited in A Bertho, op cit, p72.

41   Citied in A Bertho, op cit, p74.

42   Cited in Y Clot, 'Conduire les trains et faire grève: une conscience commune', *Futur antérieur* 33/34, p90.

43   S Béroud and J Capdevielle, op cit, p82.

44   See P Barets, op cit, p10.

45   S Béroud et al (eds), op cit, p167.

46   Cited in A Bertho, op cit, p67.

47   According to Barets, this was done more for its symbolic value than anything else.

48   See P Barets, op cit, pp24-26.

49   In this sense they represent a less developed version of the committees of action advocated by Trotsky during the struggles which took place in France during the mid-1930s. See 'For Committees of Action, Not the People's Front!', 26 November 1935, in L Trotsky, *The Crisis of the French Section 1935-36* (New York, 1977).

50   A Boulangé, 'Préparer un deuxième round', *Socialisme par en bas* 18 (April 1999).

51   J-M Pernot, op cit, p10; S Béroud and J Capdevielle, op cit, pp92-93.

52   T Negri, 'Coordination: une proposition de communisme', *Futur antérieur: les coordinations de travailleurs dans la confrontation sociale* (Paris, 1996).

53   'La charte identitaire', resolution adopted by the first SUD-PTT congress in 1989. See A Coupé and A Marchand (eds), *Sud: syndicalement incorrect/SUD-PTT une aventure collective* (Paris, 1999), pp244-245.

54   K Marx, cited in A Callinicos, *The Revolutionary Ideas of Karl Marx* (London, 1987), p148.

55   Cited in J Moreau, *Les socialistes français et le mythe révolutionnaire* (Paris, 1998), p250. For a critique of the Socialists record in office from the left, see S Halimi, *Sisyphe est Fatigué. Les Échecs de la Gauche au pouvoir* (Paris, 1993).

56   Cited in J Moreau ibid, pp272-273.

57   P Frémeaux, 'Le bilan économique des années Mitterrand', *Alternatives économiques* (June 1994).

58   S Ponthieux, 'Le développement de l'emploi à bas salaire', *L'Etat de la France 98-99* (Paris, 1998), p150.

59   A Bihr and R Pfefferkorn, *Déchiffer les inegalities* (Paris, 1999), pp44-50.

60   S Ponthieux, op cit, p150.

61   E Kouvélakis and M Vakaloulis, 'Le retour d'une affaire classée', *L'Homme et la Société* (July-December 1995), p15.

62   J Moreau, op cit, p286.

63   Ibid, pp285-286.

64   *Le Monde*, 9 October 1987. Cited in Halimi, op cit, p351.

65   *Le Point*, 30 March 1987.

66   *Le Monde*, 3 June 1997.

67   *L'Evénement du Jeudi,* 12-18 September 1991.

68   *Libération*, 3 June 1997.

69   Two smaller parties also formed part of the alliance, the left Radicals and Jean-Pierre Chevènement's Mouvement des Citoyens.

70   *Le Monde*, 28 July 1999.

71   *L'Humanité*, 4 November 1997.
72   *Le Monde*, 6 January 1998.
73   Cited in *L'Humanité*, 6 June 1997. See J Wolfreys, 'What Price Unity? The Plural Left in Office', *Contemporary Political Studies Two* (Nottingham, 1998) for initial reactions to the 1997 election.
74   *Le Monde*, 3 June 1997.
75   1 January 2000 for small businesses.
76   See J Wolfreys, op cit.
77   F Bohm, 'Les 35 heures, la loi Aubry et ses enjeux', *L'Année Sociale 1999* (Paris, 1999).
78   *Alternatives économiques* (September 1998), p22.
79   *Le Monde*, 1 September 1998.
80   *Le Monde*, 16 May 1998.
81   *Le Monde*, 19 January 1998.
82   *Le Monde*, 24 January 1998.
83   J Dubois, 'Décembre 1995: un mouvement polysémique', *Projet* 245 (Spring 1996), p106.
84   The French Socialists wanted no part of the Blair/Schröder 'Third Way' declaration made on the eve of the 1999 European elections. Minister for European affairs Pierre Moscovici told the cabinet of his astonishment on reading an early draft of the declaration, which stated that 'captains of industry deserve the same treatment as professional footballers and pop stars'. *Le Monde*, 12 June 1999.
85   Interview in *Libération*, 17 June 1999.
86   J Jaffré, 'Les élections législatives de mai-juin 1997 ou les illusions d'un scrutin', *Pouvoirs* 83 (1997), pp141-143.
87   P Perrineau, 'Les renouveaux de l'action politique', *Vingtième Siècle* 60 (Oct-Dec 1998), p114.
88   Jacques Blanc, Charles Millon, Jean-Pierre Soisson, Bernard Harang, Charles Bauer.
89   See P Fysh and J Wolfreys, *The Politics of Racism in France* (Basingstoke, 1998).
90   See ibid.
91   Le Pen's personal bodyguard, Francois Xavier-Sidos, played a leading role in the coup staged by Bob Denard's mercenary force in the Comorean Islands in September 1995.
92   B Mégret, *La flamme: Les voies de la renaissance* (Paris, 1998), pp9-10.
93   CSA-*Le Parisien*-RTL poll, *Infomatin*, 4 December 1995. Cited in M Darmon and R Rosso, *L'Après Le Pen: Enquête dans les coulisses du FN* (Paris, 1998), pp48-49.
94   *Libération*, 13 November 1997.
95   M Darmon and R Rosso, op cit, pp94-95.
96   *Le Monde*, 19 December 1997.
97   Mégret was a graduate of the Ecole Polytechnique, one of France's elite technical establishments, and had been a member of the Gaullist RPR prior to joining the Front in 1986.
98   L Trotsky, 'What is National Socialism?', 10 June 1933, in L Trotsky, *The Struggle Against Fascism in Germany* (New York, 1971), p399.
99   *Le Monde*, 18 March 1998.
100 In 1994 *Informatin* published what it claimed was a Mégretist document referring to Le Pen as a 'tyrannical has-been geriatric', *Les dossiers du Canard enchaîné*, October 1998, p64.
101 *Libération*, 14 June 1997.
102 *Le Figaro*, 2 June 1997.
103 *Le Monde*, 10 March 1998.
104 *Le Monde*, 11 April 1998. Both Calvert and Roux had retired by this time.

105 *Le Monde*, 17 June 1998.
106 *Présent*, 16 October 1998.
107 Inverview with *La Une*, November 1996. Cited in M Darmon and R Rosso, op cit, p135.
108 'Mégret-Le Pen: Le combat des chefs', in 'Mégret: Facho Devant!', *Les dossiers du Canard enchaîné* (October 1998), p63.
109 *Le Monde*, 19 November 1998.
110 According to an internal document produced by Mégret's supporters and published in *Le Monde*, 12 December 1998.
111 Le Pen himself had been banned from standing as a result of the Mantes-la-Jolie incident.
112 Internal document produced by Mégret's supporters and published in *Le Monde*, 12 December 1998.
113 *Le Monde*, 15 June 1999.
114 D Godard, 'Front National: La crise d'un parti fasciste', *Socialisme par en bas* 15 (January 1999).
115 J Pons, op cit, p24.
116 Those released in Britain include Mattieu Kassovitz's *La Haine*, about racism and the pressures of urban life on a Paris housing estate; Robert Guediguian's *Marius et Jeannette*, a sympathetic portrait of a working class quarter of Marseille; Eric Zonka's *La vie rêvée des anges*, about the friendship between two young women trapped between unemployment and dead end jobs in Lille; Sandrine Veysset's *Y-aura-t-il de la neige pour Noël?*, the story of a harsh and often brutal childhood in the south of France; and Bertrand Tavernier's unflinching depiction of a society falling apart in *It All Starts Today*.
117 L Trotsky, 'Take to the Open Sea!', in *The Crisis of the French Section 1935-36*, op cit, p75. In this instance Trotsky was referring to the need for French Trotskyists to leave the SFIO, but the general point, that revolutionaries need to respond to new situations and break with established routines, remains valid.
118 *Lutte Ouvrière*, 15 May 1998.
119 Laguiller was speaking at a public meeting organised by LO in Paris on 15 December 1995. See *Le Monde*, 18 December 1995.
120 'La situation intérieure', Texte de la majorité, *Lutte de Classe* 24 (December 1996).
121 Ibid.
122 *Lutte Ouvrière*, 17 April 1998.
123 *Le Monde*, 22 February 1997.
124 'France: combattre le Front National ou parader devant lui?', *Lutte de Classe* 27 (April 1997).
125 Lionel Jospin took part in the March 1997 demonstration against the FN congress in Strasbourg, whose mayor, the Socialist Catherine Trautman, played a prominent part in building the protest. Le Pen betrayed the extent of his anger at her during a 1997 election campaign rally when he had a cardboard effigy of her head served up to him on a plate.
126 *Lutte de Classe* 27 (April 1997).
127 *Lutte Ouvrière*, 3 April 1998.
128 This appeared in *Lutte Ouvrière*, 27 March 1998. For the LCR's response to LO's abstention, see 'Mais où était Lutte Ouvrière?' *Rouge*, 2 April 1998.
129 *Lutte Ouvrière*, 3 April 1998.
130 *Lutte de Classe* 35 (May-June 1998).
131 See D Gluckstein, *The Nazis, Capitalism and the Working Class* (London, 1999).
132 See P Fysh and J Wolfreys, op cit.
133 See, for example, *Lutte Ouvrière*, 17 April 1998.
134 *Lutte Ouvrière*, 15 May 1998.
135 C Harman, op cit.

136   Perspective of the majority tendency set out prior to the LCR's 13th congress in
       Rouge, 8 January 1998.
137   L Trotsky, 'The Mistakes of the Rightist Elements of the Communist League on
       the Trade Union Question', in *Leon Trotsky on the Trade Unions* (New York,
       1975), p37.
138   *Rouge*, 25 March 1999.
139   *Rouge*, 29 April 1999 and 20 May 1999. The LCR was involved in an abortive
       attempt to organise an anti-war demonstration for 2 June 1999
140   *Alternatives économiques* Special Issue 35 (1998), p22.
141   L Trotsky, *The First Five Years of the Comintern* (London, 1974), p354.

Nationalism and internationalism in the new Europe

PHIL MARFLEET

For most politicians in Europe the war against Serbia was justified as a mission of mercy. They declared that oppression of the Kosovans was intolerable, an appalling injustice in a region so close to their own and one requiring exemplary humanitarian action. As British prime minister Tony Blair explained to a European Union (EU) summit, 'This place Kosovo is right on the doorstep of Europe,' and Europeans were required to act in solidarity with their neighbours.[1] For Blair, principles of 'European justice' and of 'civilised society' were to be defended against national antagonism and ethnic conflict. Leaders of EU states agreed, using the summit to commit themselves to salvation of the Kosovans. The hypocrisy was breathtaking, for these same politicians had worked for years to build an EU committed to exclusion of such people, especially asylum seekers from regions on Europe's 'doorstep'. EU states had expelled tens of thousands of refugees from the Balkans and others fleeing conflicts on Europe's periphery and in the Third World. The EU excluded systematically those most in need of sanctuary, declaring them not European and therefore without rights in member states. Exclusion had in fact become a key area of collaboration between member states of the Union, to the extent that the EU had become what one newspaper called 'a club for the racially privileged'.[2] This was institutionalised racism on a continental scale: a situation starkly at odds with Blair's moral crusade and one which highlighted the contradictions of the EU and its 'Europeanism'.

The EU is routinely presented by its supporters as an internationalist project. Its founding documents refer to 'ever closer union' between peoples of the region,[3] and for decades it has been promoted as a means of overcoming national differences and state rivalries. The call to be a 'good European' therefore appeals to many on the left, who often identify the EU with modernisation, economic and social advance, and as a means of moving beyond the conflicts of the past. Social democratic and Communist parties, which have been strongly attached to national (often nationalist) agendas, have increasingly identified an internationalist dimension to the EU. Many leading figures in Socialist governments have been partisans of the Union and sometimes—like Jacques Delors, a minister in the Mitterrand government in France—they have been architects of its development. Much of the trade union leadership across Western Europe has embraced the Union, especially the 'social dimension' of the Maastricht Treaty, with its regulations on working practice and conditions which bureaucrats view as supportive of workers' rights and cross-border relationships. The British TUC, for example, moved from 'Euro-scepticism' during the 1980s to 'a deep rooted and coherent pro-European economic perspective' by the mid-1990s, and developed on ardent support for the Union as a guarantor of workers' rights.[4] Most Communist parties have followed a similar path. The Italian Communist Party (PCI) is typical of those which now see the Union as a vehicle for radical change. It has called for 'a People's Europe', not just an economic union but 'a real political entity, a real European political Union with a substantial social dimension'.[5]

For German foreign minister Joschka Fischer, the leading Green in a coalition government with the Socialist Party, the EU has taken key steps required for economic integration and is now advancing rapidly towards political union, which he views as a desirable end in itself. In January 1999 he told the European Parliament, 'Europe has already changed far more than most of our citizens have realised—a significant section of national sovereignty has been transferred.' He argued that 'political union must be our lodestar from now on'.[6]

The EU has the appearance of a body in which national differences, if not dissolved, are at least partly reconciled. Its states co-operate economically and seem to be moving towards political—even military—collaboration. Physical barriers are apparently of less importance, so that now it is possible for EU citizens to move across large areas of the continent without showing a passport. This *Schengenland*, the borderless zone created by the Schengen Treaty, now incorporates Belgium, the Netherlands, Luxembourg, France, Germany, Spain, Portugal, Italy and Austria. It is officially said by the EU to be an area of 'freedom, justice and security', yet non-EU citizens are ruthlessly excluded.[7] Such developments have encouraged arguments for 'borderless' political activity. In 1997 the British think tank Demos (which is close to New Labour) produced *Politics Without Frontiers*, a pamphlet which argued that political parties in Europe should be organised across borders because 'power has moved beyond frontiers. The time has come for politics without frontiers'.[8] According to Demos, the EU has opened possibilities for wider and deeper democracy which should be exploited by the creation of organisations operating above sectional and national interests. But the EU is not a means of collaboration for the mass of people, far less a means of developing internationalism. Its structures inhibit effective solidarity. Its 'Europeanism' is an ideology developed within the capitalist class which draws upon the same notions of national difference which leaders of the Union have apparently been so anxious to reject.

'Europeanism' is based upon the idea of 'Europeanity'—the notion that Europeans have a common heritage which sets them apart from 'others'. It is this which gives them rights in the EU—most importantly, the right of residence. For EU strategists, wider awareness of a shared European identity, and of the imagined benefits it brings, is seen as vital for successful political integration. They hope to increase popular identification with the EU and to induce consent to decisions taken through the bodies such as the European Parliament. But this notion rests upon the idea of fundamental differences between 'Europeans' and 'non-Europeans', and upon the proposition that the latter have no rights in the EU. It is on this basis that people who wish to enter EU states are excluded. Poor and vulnerable people, notably refugees, are depicted as opportunists seeking to exploit the benefits of life within the Union. At the same time, citizens of EU states are invited to identify 'internal enemies'—those depicted as out of place or even 'alien' within the New Europe. The effect is to heighten racism, weakening solidarities within the working class across the continent and between workers of Europe and others worldwide. The EU has nothing to do with internationalism, a tradition which has always been built from below, against all ideas of national and ethnic difference, and against top down 'transnationalism'.

In *The Communist Manifesto* Marx and Engels insisted that 'the working men have no country'. They argued that the nation state was alien to the interests of the proletariat and that in order to advance their interests workers must 'settle matters' with the bourgeoisie of each state, that workers must challenge the power of their 'own' capitalist class directly.[9] This opened the possibility of internationalism—assertion of 'the common interests of the whole proletariat, independently of all nationality'.[10] Internationalism implied uncompromising opposition to the local state and its dealings with the rulers of other capitalisms—other members of the 'band of warring brothers' that constituted the bourgeoisie at a world level.

It also implied practical activity by workers to organise in mutual solidarity across national borders and in solidarity with those subordinated by colonial powers. This was not a merely a matter of abstract identification with the oppressed. Marx maintained that workers must free themselves of patriotism and national superiority *in their own interests*, for without discarding these aspects of bourgeois ideology they would never themselves be free.

Marx and Engels maintained this approach throughout their political activities.[11] It was also the position taken by others who made a major contribution to Marxist theory over the next 100 years: by Luxemburg, Lenin, Trotsky and their co-thinkers. It implied opposition by revolutionary communists to the many commercial and military alliances, diplomatic pacts and deals struck by national governments. These were initiated to bring advantage to one or another section of capital, thereby damaging the interests of the exploited class. During the First World War, Rosa Luxemburg warned socialists against the idea of collaborations between European states presented as internationalist projects focused upon peace and continental harmony:

> *World peace cannot be assured through apparently utopian but basically reactionary plans, such as international arbitration by capitalist diplomats, diplomatic arrangements about 'disarmament', 'freedom of the seas' 'European communities'* [**Staatenbunde**], *'Central European customs unions', 'national buffer states' and the like. The only means of ensuring world peace is the political capacity for action and the revolutionary will of the international proletariat to throw its weight into the scales.*[12]

The comments were prophetic. Forty years later the nation states of Western Europe declared a new project for peace and mutual understanding. This European community was another 'apparently utopian' but reactionary plan—a phoney internationalism which has used the rhetoric of unity in the interests of capital.

'Tribalism'

According to the ideologues of European union, Western European society has reached an advanced stage of development which makes possible rapid integration of its national states. The region is said to have progressed from its earlier history of national rivalries, war and mutual destruction, and to be a congenial environment for all manner of collaborations. Shore sums up this view:

> *The* [EU] *is typically portrayed as a logical development of the Enlightenment:*

a force for progress inspired by science, reason, rationality and humanism. These discourses also tend to portray the European Parliament and the European Commission as heroic agents of change, leading Europe forward in search of its supposed 'federal destiny'.[13]

This is the official interpretation of the origins, role and historic task of Europe and of today's Union. It suggests that the EU is a higher form of organisation, the development of which has been facilitated by far-sighted economic and political strategists. According to this view, comments Michel Lowy, 'Western Europe is presented as a harmonious world, well beyond irrational passions. Reconciled, the nations of this democratic and modern part of the continent are quickly moving towards their integration in a united European Community'.[14] The EU is often contrasted with eastern Europe, especially with the efflorescence of national movements and 'ethnicised' ideologies in the Balkan region. In a typical observation, the leading Eurocrat Jacques Attali describes the Balkans as afflicted by 'tribalism'. Western Europe, with superior modes of social and political organisation, should fear its influence, he maintains, for 'Balkan tribalism' may spread like a contagion. Attali is worried that, 'We [Western Europeans] have only a limited time to stop the slide towards tribalism before it engulfs eastern Europe and quite possibly takes us with it'.[15] The theme of a harmonious Union is taken up by many academics, even those who strongly reject the notion of 'essential' superiority of Western European society. Ernst Gellner, for example, has argued that developments in Western Europe have already diminished conflict in the region. As a result of 'economic and cultural convergence [which] jointly diminish ethnic hostilities', he maintains, nationalism in the region is now 'relatively benign'.[16]

But 'ethnic hostilities' in Western Europe have not diminished; rather they have been generalised across the region and formalised by the EU itself. While Eurocrats and politicians in member states have declared for internationalism and harmony, they have simultaneously organised a regime of exclusion which divides 'Europeans' from 'non-Europeans' as effectively as any imagined differences which were earlier said to separate Germans, French, British or Italians. Their 'Fortress Europe' in fact draws upon ideas which earlier underpinned Europe's rival nationalisms. It has encouraged racism in general and helped to provide rationales for the extreme right, where the vocabulary of Nazism has reappeared in the form of demands for 'living space' and talk of the 'European home'.

Since the mid-1980s, when the EU began to construct its exclusionary regime, the idea of securing Europe against 'threats' from without and from within has become more general. By the late 1990s, with a 'harmonised' migration policy in place, EU states were focused intently upon removing migrants and others deemed 'bogus', 'clandestine' or 'illegal'. The vast majority of those targeted were poor and vulnerable people, almost invariably of African, Asian, Latin American or Middle Eastern origin. But EU states have also targeted an 'enemy' long present within European territorial boundaries. Roma people were identified by fascist movements of the 1920s and 1930s as one of their two greatest enemies: at least 200,000 *Zigeuner* (Gypsies) were sent to the death camps.[17] They have recently faced new persecution, especially in areas of eastern and south eastern Europe in which the collapse of state capitalism has been followed by increased inequality, immiseration and social dislocation.[18] Kenrick notes that renewed anti-Roma activity comes at a time when commemorations of the Holocaust have been taking place across Europe: 'As we recall the events of the Nazi period, it is shocking to see the beginnings of a new genocide against Gypsies in eastern Europe. Romanies have replaced the Jews as scapegoats for real or imagined ills of the majority population'.[19]

This persecution is not restricted to eastern Europe. Roma refugees from the Czech Republic, Slovakia, Hungary and Romania who have sought asylum in Western Europe have been subject to media attack and to assaults by racists. Most have been expelled—returned to countries in which they are increasingly vulnerable. In a chilling reminder of the cynicism with which racists and the British state responded to anti-Semitism in Europe in the 1930s, Roma arriving in Britain have faced a strident campaign for their removal. In 1998 Roma refugees claiming asylum were described in the press as 'bootleggers', 'scum of the earth' and 'human sewage'. A headline in one local paper urged action: 'We Want To Wash The Dross Down The Drain'.[20] The Refugee Council comments that this was not just the work of a few rogue journalists in the provincial press but was a 'media pogrom': 'Apart from a handful of articles which attempted to look beyond the caricature of the wandering Gypsy ever on the lookout to rip off the honest taxpayer, coverage was unremittingly hostile, hysterical, and in specific cases directly incendiary of racial hatred. Hostility was carried across from the tabloid press to the broadsheets: indeed, *The Independent* newspaper carried one of the worst "attack" headlines, shouting "Gypsies Invade Dover Hoping For A Handout".'[21]

Following firebombings on houses in which the refugees were staying and demonstrations by fascist groups, and despite solidarity from the Anti Nazi League, the Roma were soon deported. The role of the British government demonstrated how hollow is talk of 'harmony' within and among Western European states. In full knowledge of the circumstances faced by the Roma in eastern Europe, the Labour government declared them to be 'bogus' asylum seekers who intended to 'abuse the system'. Heads of Roma households were imprisoned en masse—in effect, interned—in a policy described by the Refugee Council as 'crude and cruel'.[22] Meanwhile British immigration minister Mike O'Brien appeared on TV in the Czech Republic to spell out that further Roma asylum seekers arriving in Britain would indeed be seized and deported: this from a minister also responsible within the government for 'race relations'.

Roma asylum seekers arriving in France, Austria and Spain later met a similar fate. Across Western Europe communities fleeing intensified oppression were greeted with the same hostility by a series of states mobilising a common asylum policy—the EU's 'harmonised' asylum regime. So too with refugees from other regions. By the mid-1990s, a network of prison camps and holding centres had been established across the EU, especially along the southern borders of the Union, where frontiers were said to be 'permeable'. Here, thousands of asylum seekers were held. Over a few weeks in mid-1998 the Italian government alone seized, incarcerated and later deported 15,000 asylum seekers, most to North African states.[23] In a sickening parallel to the attacks on Roma in Britain, right wing MPs in Italy took the opportunity to call for immigrants to be tattooed with identification codes—a blatant reference to Nazi practices which spelt out how official racism encourages the fascists.[24] This is the reality against which Eurocrats' and politicians' smug talk of a continent integrated by 'European values' and of 'social peace' should be tested. It makes true collaboration between workers' movements and solidarity with the oppressed more urgent.

'Rescue of the nation state'

EU propaganda depicts a happy transnational Europe in which old conflicts are being erased. As Lowy argues, these notions of a benign EU are absurd: they make for 'an idyllic image, an illusion, if not a mystification'.[25] This ideological representation of the EU has emerged from politicians' increasingly desperate attempts to maintain a project which has been riven with contradictions from the beginning.

The EU had its origins in attempts to stabilise European capitalism in the wake of the Second World War. At the end of hostilities, the victorious capitalist classes were at first concerned to prevent recovery of the German state and in the process to enrich themselves. The US, USSR, Britain and France set about pillaging German industry, dismantling the most advanced plants and re-erecting them hundreds or thousands miles away; according to the British government, this was essential for 'denazification'.[26] When Moscow's intention to incorporate Eastern Europe became plain, however, a new approach was adopted. US strategists concluded that the USSR was to be America's main rival in the battle for global dominance. Their Cold

War logic dictated that the Western Allies should quickly consolidate their portion of the German economy and stabilise areas of European capitalism which had not come under Stalinist rule. In 1947 the US proposed the Marshall Plan to provide support for Western Europe and as the means to rearm the region in alliance with Washington. In 1948 this was followed by establishment of the North Atlantic Treaty Organisation (NATO), which mobilised North American and Western European states against the USSR and its satellites.

The first new grouping was the Organisation of European Economic Co-operation, which all states wishing to receive Marshall Aid were compelled to join. Problems soon became evident: local capitalist classes continued to pursue mutual rivalries and there was general suspicion of Germany. The French state proposed two collaborative schemes which it hoped would advance its own interests: the Schuman Plan for a 'Europeanised' coal and steel industry, and the Pleven Plan for a transnational army. The latter failed but the Schuman Plan produced the European Coal and Steel Community (ECSC), which for 15 years from 1952 facilitated a recovery of European heavy industry while restricting the independent growth of a key sector of German capitalism.

The ECSC expressed the pattern of accommodation and competition which characterised relations between European capitalisms during this period. This reflected the awareness of national capitalist classes that they had growing interests which transcended frontiers but that each was located firmly within structures of a specific state. The European Economic Community (EEC), established in 1957, was a further move towards collaboration but not one which subordinated interests of the state to a supranational ideal or a vision of co-operation. As the long boom of the world system continued into the 1960s, allowing unprecedented levels of growth, core EEC states (Germany in particular) were beneficiaries of more open access to the European market. This was De Gaulle's *Europe des patries*—a liaison of capitalist classes seeking advantage through co-operation *and* competition. Twenty years after the Second World War, European capitalisms had fallen behind their global rivals but appeared to be far more robust than in the period of post-war chaos. It is in this sense that Milward has described the EEC/EU as 'the European rescue of the nation state'.[27]

Alex Callinicos describes the EEC of the 1960s as a contradictory formation, 'caught between the conflicting tendencies for the internationalisation and the national organisation of capital'.[28] It was being shaped by specific tendencies within world capitalism, producing a structure which was unstable and especially prone to crisis and to tensions between member states and between various factions of capital. It was not, as ideologues of the Union have claimed, a development towards continental integration based upon collaboration of peoples said to share a European cultural heritage or a common 'identity'.

What is 'Europe'?

Rietbergen comments that the notion of 'Europe' has always been elusive:

> *What is Europe? It is, of course, wrong to consider it as a 'natural fact', to call it a continent and to attribute to it the specious security of a distinct geographical entity, as so often happens. If anything, Europe is a political and cultural concept, invented and experienced by an intellectual elite.*[29]

Ideas about Europe and Europeans did not take a definite political/cultural shape until the 18th century. Then the idea of a common continental heritage emerged as part of the consolidation of national ideologies which were associated with the rise of the capitalist state. Many leading Enlightenment thinkers suggested that European peoples shared traditions and ideals which set them apart from others. Voltaire, for example, maintained, 'Today, there are no longer Frenchmen, Germans, Spaniards, even Englishmen, there are only Europeans'.[30] Such notions reflected some of the common experiences of the European bourgeoisies (especially commercial capitalists) in the wider world. As the main beneficiaries of colonial expansion, they drew readily upon ideas of a European 'civilisation' said to be dynamic, progressive and morally superior, and which provided rationales for the subordination of peoples they viewed as backward and inferior. To this extent, the idea of Europe was one generated by those who wished to assert a universal mission for capitalism.

The 'Europeanism' suggested in these approaches was contradictory. The colonising powers were fierce rivals and ideas about 'Europe' primarily served national ideologies. The Dutch historian Pim den Boer suggests that, although the idea of Europe now became much more significant, 'various groupings had their own idea of what Europe had been and what it ought to be'.[31] Delanty comments that, in the case of France, 'as far as the concept of Europe is concerned, it was a thoroughly French affair and proclaimed "the superiority of the European religion, the white race and the French language".'[32] The pan-continental vision was inextricably linked to the activities of capitalist classes for whom the nation state was a key framework for competitive activity.[33]

Ideas about Europe which accommodated specific nationalisms in this way dominated until well into the 20th century.[34] Then one current rapidly gained prominence: the idea of an 'essential', unified continent, in which local differences were merely superficial and should be set aside in the quest for a unity of nations. This fascist vision focused intently upon local nationalism but also maintained that the local state would be transcended as Europe was unified in pursuit of a historic mission to impose world order. Europeans were deemed to possess elemental qualities which placed them above others, hence Hitler's Thousand Year Reich was presented as a 'European Order' rather than a German Reich. As part of this project, European society was to be cleansed of the 'alien' presence and would advance towards its task of subordinating 'Asiatic' and other influences worldwide. Delanty comments that such a vision can be seen as 'the apotheosis of the idea of Europe'.[35]

Europe and the West

After the Second World War, Europe was divided among the victorious states. Each of the post-war superpowers declared the fascist vision intolerable and asserted that the future of the continent lay with their own models of social order: Washington's liberal capitalism or Moscow's Communism. American energies went mainly into engagement with Europe at the economic and military levels but at the same time its Cold War warriors began a battle for ideas which centred on the construction of a specific image of Europe, a region now held to be linked inextricably with the West. This was an urgent task, for the experiences of capitalist crisis followed by war, and then by promises of peace and reconstruction, had intensified class struggle. The masses were in a radical mood. In Germany invading armies had been directed to destroy a workers' movement based on shop committees and councils.[36] In Italy workers had seized factories in the northern cities. In France they had set up local committees and conducted purges of wartime collaborators; in elections the Communist Party won five million votes and sent 161 deputies to parliament.[37] In Britain workers' rising confidence was reflected in a crushing Labour victory over the Tories.

Invariably it was the strategy of Communist and Socialist parties which saved ruling classes from further crisis, surrendering possibilities of a genuine internationalism. Nonetheless, such developments caused consternation among the rulers of Europe and in the US, where attempts to develop a global strategy to assure American hegemony were now well under way. Expressing a preoccupation among American strategists, one US analyst commented that the situation in Europe required 'ideological combat', for 'our principal weakness is not economic or military but ideological—of ideas'.[38]

The main thrust of systematic propaganda conducted by the US and its allies was to distance post-war European society from the recent experience of economic crisis, unemployment, fascism and war—and from ideas about political alternatives identified with the superpower to the east. This was to be achieved by developing new fictions about Europe and its destiny, what Burgess calls 'a new non-racial [non-Nazi] self identity for Western society'.[39] The Europe to be depicted in official propaganda, in the media, and the education system, was a Western Europe made to stand in an imagined tradition of classical influences, high culture, economic advance and political liberalism. Meanwhile, the 'East', including Eastern Europe, was identified with backwardness, authoritarianism and repression. Churchill's metaphor of the Iron Curtain was used to separate the continent in two senses: physically, along the borders of Poland, Czechoslovakia and the two Germanies, and politically/culturally, by suggesting that the social character of each zone was distinct. Ruling classes of the Stalinist bloc, locked into economic and military competition with the US, responded to every ideological gambit with their own, intensifying the propaganda battle.

Areas west of the East/West border now fell within the North Atlantic, a region invented in order to link Europe with its guardian capitalism in the US. Enormous efforts went into inventing traditions of Western civilisation said to be shared by (Western) Europe and North America. Academic study of the East focused on 'totalitarianism', with an often explicit message that fascism and communism were intimately related and were to be contrasted with the liberal democracy of the 'true' (Western) European tradition and of North America. This revisionism centred upon forgetting all that had just been learned by the mass of people about capitalist crisis and its consequences in Europe. It denied that fascism had its origins in the western regions of Europe where significant sections of the bourgeoisie had facilitated its rise and had sometimes participated in its most barbaric practices. These same classes were busy ensuring business as usual, their activities supported by the US. There were difficulties in maintaining the new perspective: for example, in accommodating Franco's fascism within the vision of Western democracy and of incorporating Turkey (of 'the East') within NATO. The fiction was nevertheless maintained: Delanty comments that, at an ideological level, 'Europe had in effect become America's eastern frontier'.[40]

Rotten heart of Europe

By the 1980s the EEC (later declared the European Community (EC) and in 1993 the EU) was considered an unprecedented success. For the western half of the continent, suggests former Eurocrat Bernard Connolly, Pax Americana had brought 'unparalleled prosperity, stability and democratic legitimacy'.[41] Britain had been the only major state eligible for membership not to have joined. Here a specific pattern of capitalist development had left the ruling class uncertain about its geo-strategic interests but in 1973 even the British had opted in.[42] Increasingly European capitalists sought to collaborate in ways they hoped would give them an advantage within the global system, especially *vis-à-vis* newly industrialising countries such as those of East Asia. Martiniello comments that the priority of the EC was 'to complete the internal market as soon as possible and to assure the conditions of its efficiency'.[43]

But the old contradictions remained. Collaboration was accompanied by rivalries and sometimes by prolonged conflict between member states. The EC had also become a forum for competition between politicians who hoped to gain support at home by championing specific national agendas around all manner of European issues—exchange rates, agricultural quotas, fishing rights, commercial standards, military relations. At the most inconsequential level, hundreds of hours of debate in EC forums were taken up in disputes over the contents of the European sausage, or definitions of chocolate. More fundamental disagreements over the allocation of vast sums of money from EC budgets or over monetary policy put the most powerful states at loggerheads for years. For Connolly, the whole enterprise was carried out in an atmosphere of 'mutual distrust and suspicion' so intense as to subvert the notion of union and to constitute 'the rotten heart of Europe'.[44]

By the mid-1980s European capitalism as a whole was facing problems which magnified contradictions in the EC. The long boom of the world system which had fuelled post-war recovery was long since over. A global recession in the early 1970s had been followed by a further crisis which now sharply reduced growth rates. There were vigorous attempts to re-organise traditional sectors of major European economies: some—such as the British coal industry—were largely eliminated. Everywhere unemployment rose, while most governments attempted to reduce state spending, prompting increased working class resistance. Governments became preoccupied by domestic difficulties; at the same time they turned more systematically to the EC for support. In particular, they sought financial stability through association with the strongest of the European economies, Germany. European currencies were linked through the Exchange Rate Mechanism (ERM) to the Deutschmark, making the Bundesbank in effect a European central bank. This had the effect of generalising developments in the German economy across the EC, and by the mid-1980s, with the German economic 'miracle' at an end and unemployment rising, other economies were quickly affected. There was increased hostility to the EC from some factions of capital in several states, notably in Britain, where Europhobe elements in the Conservative Party began a campaign of strident opposition. A sense of crisis developed within the structures of the EC. There was a loss of confidence in the old vision of integration, summed up by Connolly as a new 'Europessimism'.[45]

Eurocrats were also worried that they faced a general crisis of legitimacy among people of member states. They suggested that the EC's *raison d'être*, its agenda for economic integration, was inadequate to stimulate popular identification with the Community, especially at a time of recession. The EC was not a nation state in which an ideology of 'belonging' could be mobilised during periods of instability or crisis. It lacked a framework for nationalism: myths of common origin, a national religious community, a monarchy. The Community had been constructed upon nation states which had emerged from centuries of local rivalry: there could be no reference point for an EC patriotism, no European Jeanne d'Arc. Waever and Kelstrup note the rising anxiety among 'worried Eurocrats [who] fear that there are limits as to how far one can push integration in the political and economic spheres unless people feel sufficiently European'.[46] The Community seemed to be suffering from an 'ideological deficit': as the senior Eurocrat Jacques Delors commented, 'people do not fall in love with an Inner Market'.[47]

One index of official concern about these issues was the creation at this period of the 'Eurobarometer'—a complex polling system designed to measure mass attitudes towards the EC. Martiniello comments that this amounted to the 'creation of a tool to control evolution of "European public opinion" at the same time as it was trying to give birth to it'.[48] The modest symbolism of the EEC which had emerged in 1960s and 1970s—that of 'balloons and flags'[49]—now seemed inadequate. Eurocrats, pro-EU politicians and academics began to actively investigate the idea of promoting 'Europeanity' or 'Europeanness'—a Europe for the mass of people of the member states. They wished to stimulate what the European Commission itself called 'a feeling of belonging to the European construction'.[50] This, it hoped, would amount to a substantial sense of being 'European' by means of 'central elements of identification to the European Community'.[51]

The twin problems of feuding among member states and of the EC's crisis of legitimacy were partly resolved by close collaboration in one area in which states could find common ground—that of immigration. From the mid-1980s a number of secretive inter-governmental meetings between ministers and senior Eurocrats developed policy on immigration and asylum. This was the basis of the Schengen Agreement discussed above. In a further series of agreements, notably the Dublin Convention of 1990, member states put in place draconian measures against migrants and asylum seekers. By the early 1990s a Fortress Europe had been constructed, within which those identified as European were permitted to reside, and from which most others were to be excluded.

As early as 1989 Cohen and Joly commented that European

governments 'bicker endlessly about lamb imports, agricultural subsidies, monetary policy and the potential shape of a possible political union', but that a uniform migration policy had 'quietly emerged'. They concluded that 'the European Community looks more and more like a gilded cage with ministers of the interior bracing and painting the bars'.[52] Those to remain outside were migrants from regions adjoining Western Europe and from the Third World. For decades they had been subject to restriction and most were now to be excluded from the EU as a whole. Any doubts about rights of entry were to be resolved by a new definition of citizenship of the Union. Martiniello comments that the measures constituted formalisation by the EC of a new 'ethno-racial conception of European society'.[53]

Living space

Although the EU could not mobilise a national ideology, it drew upon the nationalist traditions of European states and in particular upon the ideas of a resurgent right. Economic crisis had opened opportunities for fascism to re-emerge in a series of countries.[54] In France the National Front (FN) recorded a vote of just 0.3 percent in 1979; by 1984 this had increased to almost 11 percent and the FN had won a large parliamentary representation.[55] By 1988 it had become a significant national force, with veteran fascist leader Jean-Marie Le Pen winning some 15 percent of votes in the first round of the presidential elections.[56] In Germany a clutch of smaller parties rose to prominence. The Republican Party (REP), the National Democratic Party (NDP) and the German People's Union (DVU) all recorded big gains: by 1991 the DVU was able to secure over 10 percent of the vote in local elections in some major cities.[57] Meanwhile more ambiguous populist movements, such as the Austrian Freedom Party, the Flemish Vlaams Blok, and in Italy the Northern Leagues, made dramatic advances.

These organisations campaigned on racist agendas, mainly on the impact of recession and the imagined threat of non-Europeans to national states and to Europe as a whole. In France the FN led with the slogan, 'Two million immigrants equals two million unemployed'.[58] Its main target was people of North African origin alleged by the Front to have stolen French jobs and to be threatening the good health of French society. According to Le Pen, migrants undermined the purity of France and of Europe as a whole. Evans sums up the FN perspective: 'North Africans must go back to North Africa; the cultural superiority of Western Europe must be affirmed; all [racial] intermingling must stop; in short there must be a return to the colonial order of things'.[59] The REP made a similar connection between immigration and economic crisis, portraying Germany as a boat overflowing with migrants who were sucking the German economy dry. An REP poster declared that 'Germany cannot accept any more foreigners because the boat is full'.[60] German fascists identified Roma as a special enemy, describing them as part of a 'Gypsy plague', while they targeted non-Europeans in general, calling upon Germans to take the 'immigrant problem' into their own hands.[61] Evans comments that the imagery peddled by the DVU and REP, of a beleaguered national identity under threat from foreigners, had precise outcomes: there was a huge increase in racist violence.[62]

In a crisis stricken Europe images of the past were returning. It was soon clear that the extreme right was able to influence mainstream bourgeois parties which feared that they were being undercut by a more assertive populism. This was especially marked where fascist and crypto-fascist organisations had a presence in national or regional governments. In France centre-right currents such as the Union for French Democracy (UDF) were easily affected. The UDF candidate for mayor in Marseilles ran a campaign under the slogan 'Marseilles for the Marseillais'.[63] In Toulon the UDF mayor argued:

[France] *was never supposed to have a role as a refuge for the unemployed of Africa and Europe. Our country has become a dustbin for all the collection of revolutionaries, delinquents and anarchists of all types. We should kick them out.*[64]

The reformist left was also influenced. The Socialist Party candidate for mayor of Paris attacked the media for 'frightening' voters by carrying images of 'dark skinned faces' which antagonised the 'domestic electorate'.[65] Meanwhile the Communist Party had already led protests against what it called dumping of African migrants in the Parisian suburbs. Fysh and Wolfreys comment that this 'helped to legitimise the central plank of the FN programme'.[66] The impact on government policy was plain to see. Wihtol de Wenden comments that migration policies had been discussed earlier in the context of economic objectives, or 'clothed in technocratic discourse':

Immigration policies are now formed in response to the collective insecurities and imaginings of public opinion; the clampdown on illegal immigrants, the need for tighter border controls, the threat of delinquency and of religious fundamentalism, the perceived loss of French identity, and the fears of demographic invasion are characteristic reactions.[67]

One striking aspect of the right wing revival was the use of fascist notions of an earlier era, such as that of the 'pollution' of Europe and the notion of 'living space'. In Germany the REP argued that access to Germany must be restricted to Germans; its leader, Franz Schönhuber, declaimed: 'We're not a welfare office for the Mediterranean. We want to protect the German people's ecological living space against foreign infiltration'.[68] The notion of 'space' recalled Nazi campaigns of expansion and of extermination but was now given a new gloss. In public statements neo-Nazis talked less about biological difference and the importance of 'race' than about 'culture' and 'cultural space'. This was consistent with a shift within the fascist discourse from a focus on 'scientific racism' to ideas about ethnicity and the ethnic group. A new fascist 'culturalism' emphasised people's common identities, said to be formed in a common 'space'. Le Pen argued, 'Nature assigns all living things living zones suitable for their aptitudes and affinities. The same is true of men and peoples'.[69] He concluded, 'We must act by occupying our vital space, because nature has a horror of space and if we do not occupy it, others will occupy it in our place'.[70]

The charge against European governments and against the EU is that in constructing new policies on migration and on asylum they drew upon nationalisms which were strongly influenced by such ideas. This is not to suggest that bourgeois parties shared the fascists' agenda. They had independently reached the conclusion that it was necessary to mobilise populist rhetoric to ameliorate the effects of crisis and that they should construct a Fortress Europe. But they calculatedly used the language and national symbolism of the extreme right, appearing to endorse fascist demands and to give legitimacy to Le Pen, Schönhuber and their supporters. Delors had long attacked critics of the EU who summoned the earlier history of European nationalism against the Union, deriding them as 'those who awaken phantoms'.[71] But now the EU was borrowing from these traditions to define itself as a community of exclusion, establishing all manner of measures to identify, seize and expel those who illegitimately entered 'the European space'.

In a study of the development of migration policy in the EU, the Minority Rights Group concludes that before the mid-1980s it was not possible to speak of a 'European policy'. By the end of the decade this had become 'one of the central issues deserving special declarations, resolutions and policy formation. All the main European bodies [took] it up and some were created specially for that purpose'.[72] For the EC this outcome was entirely satisfactory. Immigration had provided a unique area of co-operation among member states and appeared to show that, despite the problems faced by local capitalisms, and despite the resentments, rivalries and chaos associated with economic, commercial and financial strategy, the Community could still be made to 'work'. Although it was not a nation state, the EC was already mimicking the state ideologically, producing a Europeanism constructed from the materials of nationalism.

Doomsday

The collapse of the Stalinist regimes in the late 1980s gave added impetus to the quest for 'Europeanity'. Rationales for a Europe defined by reference to the East/West divide were gone. The Cold War had fixed both the territorial and political/cultural frontiers of Western Europe. At a time when its internal problems seemed almost insurmountable, the Union had lost its Communist bogey and key reference point. EU ideologues turned almost immediately to a new imagined threat: that of the inundation of Western Europe by unwanted migrants.

Castles and Miller note, 'By 1990 a new spectre haunted Europe: that of an influx from the East. In Western Europe there was speculation about mass migration on a scale not seen since the collapse of the Roman Empire'.[73] Official reports suggested that tens of millions of people freed from Stalinist rule were ready to trek westwards. In 1991 the Council of Europe commented that 'Western European countries [are] disturbed—in some cases terrified—by the prospect of migration from countries of the former Eastern bloc'.[74] EU countries promptly reached deals with eastern neighbours, including Poland, the Czech Republic and Slovakia, providing 'aid' in return for undertakings that the latter would act as buffer states to keep the expected hordes at bay. Meanwhile, Italian and Austrian troops were deployed to counter the perceived threat of migratory Roma communities, judged to be the greatest menace.[75] In effect, EU states bolstered the old East/West frontier, the very borderline they had long depicted as a symbol of Stalinist tyranny. But there was no mass migration, for, as Burgess observes, 'fear of foreign numbers [was] an expression of Western anxieties, not Eastern realities'.[76]

The collapse of the East had not brought a new European dawn in which the EC project could flourish. The capitalisms of Europe were soon suffering from the impact of a further world recession, the third since the early 1970s. They were said to be afflicted by 'Eurosclerosis' and to be increasingly inefficient and uncompetitive *vis-à-vis* global rivals, principally the US and the then booming tiger economies of East Asia. The unification of Germany had had unexpected outcomes: expansion of state spending had been followed by a clampdown that generalised recession across the EU. Working class resistance again intensified, especially in France, Italy and Germany, where major strikes forced government concessions. At the same time, the right wing revival continued. As member states entered negotiations over the Maastricht Treaty, which was intended to speed up economic integration, the

Community was more insecure and divided. In 1992 the ERM effectively collapsed and the prospect of further integration looked increasingly implausible. Callinicos describes the EC at this period as less an effective collaboration than a 'bizarre European amalgam of supranational institutions and intergovernmental co-operation'.[77] Such legitimacy as the EU possessed was widely questioned: one expression of the problem was the number of academic projects set up to investigate 'Europeanity' and 'European identity',[78] together with increased interest in the Eurobarometer.[79]

The crisis of the 1980s had produced an EC focused upon migration control, and that of the 1990s intensified these concerns. This was the only area in which the Community advanced as its partisans wished. The Maastricht Treaty of 1992 aimed 'to strengthen the protection of the rights and interests of its Member States through the introduction of a citizenship of the Union'. The wording was significant: it was not the interests of people but of states that was central. Article 8.2 declared, 'Every person holding the nationality of a Member State shall be a citizen of the Union.' The EC set about excluding all those not embraced by the new definition. It now enacted further measures on migration and asylum, producing what Joly calls 'a coherent and watertight body of policies'.[80] These were promptly directed towards another region seen as a source of threat: North Africa.

In 1991 the Western European Union warned of new migrations from the south that were likely to affect Europe's economic health and political stability, while an EC report alerted member states to the implications of a 'population explosion' in the Maghreb. Collinson remarks that these and other analyses generated a mood of alarm in official EC circles: 'a growing paranoia complex in Western Europe which centred on apocalyptic images of a Europe under siege'.[81] Lister comments that North African countries were now 'frequently referred to by [European] Commission officials, politicians and academics as a "threat", a "population bomb" or "time bomb".'[82] She notes that these phrases echoed those used in the 1960s book *The Population Bomb* by Paul Ehrlichs—a neo-Malthusian analysis of developments in the Third World which predicted that uncontrolled reproduction of peoples of Africa, Asia and Latin America would result in mass starvation and global disorder. Lister comments, 'It is worth recalling that this book had significant racist and sexist undertones'.[83] Its vocabulary was nonetheless shamelessly borrowed by Eurocrats and academics.[84]

What *The Guardian* called a 'doomsday metaphor' was conjured up by EU officials.[85] They portrayed Western Europe as a target for tens of millions of unwanted people from the south, whose presence would destabilise societies seen as prosperous and harmonious. There was indeed a mass of evidence to show that repeated crises of the world system had had a serious impact in many areas of the Third World. The great majority of refugees, however, moved into neighbouring regions. A fraction of migrants reached Europe: during the second half of the 1980s the increase in asylum applications to states in the EC represented under 5 percent of the total rise in numbers of refugees worldwide.[86] The pattern did not change radically. By the mid-1990s the number of refugees in Africa, Asia and Latin America dwarfed the numbers in Western Europe. In Uganda there was one refugee for every 93 of the total population; in Iran 1:29; in Guinea 1:16; in Lebanon 1:11; and in Malawi 1:10. By contrast, the combined total of refugees and asylum seekers in Germany was 1:633; in France 1:2,876; in Britain 1:3,431; and in Italy 1:33,300.[87] The EU nonetheless continued relentlessly to depict Western Europe as a region in imminent danger from the migrant hordes.

Green menace

The principal 'threat' was not only that of the number of imagined migrants but the danger presented by their culture. The rise of religious activism since the Iranian Revolution had given Islam a higher political profile at a world level; the new development was to impute to all Muslims the beliefs, aims and strategies of 'fundamentalism', which was portrayed as an elemental threat to European culture. The media routinely carried analyses of a global Islamic menace, with Europe depicted as a target zone for migrants who would make common cause with resident Muslim communities increasingly depicted as a fifth column within European society.

This was not a novel scenario. The Orientalist tradition had long depicted societies of 'the East' as backward, perverse, menacing and inferior.[88] The colonial venture in the Middle East and Asia had mobilised such perspectives as a key element in its ideologies of domination. In the early 1990s these were revitalised, mainly by conservative American academics seeking to identify a new world enemy which could provide a reference point for US imperialism. Cold War warriors such as Huntington, Krauthammer and Pipes replaced the Communist Red Menace with a Green Menace (green being the colour of Islam). For Huntington, Islam, with its 'bloody borders', was now the main threat to Western Europe and North America.[89] For Pipes, Islam should be seen as a new totalitarianism:

> *Fundamentalist Islam is a radical utopian movement closer in spirit to other such movements (communism, fascism) than to traditional religion. By nature*

anti-democratic and aggressive, anti-Semitic and anti-Western, it has great plans. Indeed, spokesmen for fundamentalist Islam see their movement standing in direct competition to Western civilisation and challenging it for global supremacy.[90]

The proposition that Islamic activism equalled fascism/communism was absurd. It was nonetheless absorbed by many partisans of the EU. Willy Claes, Belgian prime minister and later NATO chief, placed the new threat of Islam precisely in the space vacated by the Red Menace:

Muslim fundamentalism is at least as dangerous as Communism once was. Please do not underestimate this risk...at the conclusion of this age it is a serious threat, because it represents terrorism, religious fanaticism and exploitation of social and economic justice.[91]

Other leading European politicians pursued a similar approach. In France the leading conservative, Jacques Chirac, complained of an 'overdose' of foreigners, targeting Muslims and blacks.[92] In an analysis of anti-Muslim sentiment across Western Europe, Bjorgo comments upon the link between attitudes to Islam in general and hostility towards Muslim communities: 'Even among political elites, Islam is more and more replacing Communism as the perceived main threat to Western civilisation'.[93]

Alarmist pronouncements about the Islamic threat appeared in the mainstream European press. In Britain Charles Moore, editor of *The Spectator* and later of *The Daily Telegraph*, declared:

You can be British without speaking English or being Christian or being white, but nevertheless Britain is basically English speaking, Christian and white, and if one starts to think that it might become basically Urdu speaking and Muslim and brown, one gets frightened and angry. Because of our obstinate refusal to have enough babies, Western European civilisation will start to die at the point when it could have been revived with new blood. Then the hooded hordes will win, and the Koran will be taught, as Gibbon famously imagined, in the schools of Oxford.[94]

Moore's lament for new blood echoed Le Pen's assertion that the body of Europe must defend itself against the 'virus' of Islam, with the FN as a 'natural defence mechanism' which had sprung forth to protect French identity.[95] Meanwhile, the popular press produced attacks on Muslims that would not have been out of place in fascist publications. Cartoon depictions of Islam—hooded, veiled, violent—often with bloody sword in hand— became a tabloid genre.[96] These developments were so marked that the term Islamophobia was coined to capture the idea of fear or dislike of Muslims in general.

It was against this background that the EU moved towards an unprecedented foreign policy initiative. In 1995 all the EU foreign ministers met their counterparts from Middle East and North African states at Barcelona. Their purpose, said Spanish foreign minister (later also NATO chief) Javier Solana, was to deal with 'a kind of paranoia' about threats emanating from the Middle East which was abroad in Europe. The Barcelona Agreement which emerged to deal with this problem was an astonishing document. It promised vast sums of money (some 7 billion Ecu—about £5 billion) to Middle Eastern states, ostensibly to assist their development and to stimulate fraternal relations across the Mediterranean region. In order to mobilise this money, the EU virtually liquidated its aid budget to other areas of the world, including the most needy African states. By the end of the decade this had had the effect of reversing the EU's entire development policy.[97] The quid pro quo, evident only in the small print of the agreement, was an undertaking by these states to stop migration and to use all measures to inhibit the Islamic movements.

Following the Barcelona deal, the EU moved to close its 'leaking' southern borders. Immigration officials' main anxiety was the 'permeability' of Greece and Italy, whose long coastlines on the Union's southern borders were being 'violated' by thousands of refugees from conflicts in the Balkans and the Middle East. A series of disasters at sea, in which hundreds of refugees drowned off the Italian coast, highlighted what *The Guardian* called 'trafficking across the moat of Fortress Europe'.[98] The EU was less concerned with the refugees' fate than with pressuring Italy and Greece to police the moat effectively. Italy was compelled to introduce new laws in line with the Schengen provisions and to intercept the 'illegals'. Those denied entry to Italy were placed in prison in camps in Puglia and in Sicily. In July 1998 alone 3,000 were intercepted and incarcerated; following riots at a camp in Agrigento, police fired on refugees, injuring at least ten.[99] Meanwhile, Spain set out to plug gaps in the EU's southernmost border around the Spanish enclaves of Melilla and Ceuta in Morocco. Fences ten feet high and dotted with sensors, cameras and control towers were put in place to prevent onward movement into Spain, while Spanish forces were deployed to put down riots at a 'reception centre' in the city.[100] The EU has indeed been fortified against those portrayed as a threat to its citizens. In fact threats to the mass of people in member states come from elsewhere—from their historic class adversaries who established the EU and are determined to make workers pay the cost of further integration of the Union.

Class logic

Miles notes that Fortress Europe has a class character, being 'intended to deny entry to almost all of those seeking a buyer for their semi- and unskilled labour power, as well as those seeking sanctuary from civil conflict and repression'. He concludes that 'there is a predominant class logic to the structure of exclusion'.[101]

The vast majority of those denied entry are poor and vulnerable; those with wealth and privilege are invariably admitted. People who wish to enter the EU from Middle East states repeatedly find that proof of a well padded bank account produces a visa to visit London, Paris or Rome for shopping. Most other requests are refused. Business people usually move freely across the Union and those who face difficulties can buy their way in. In the early 1990s British passports were being offered legally to Hong Kong businessmen for £60,000. In 1999 it was revealed that Conservative Party treasurer Michael Ashcroft had been selling Belizean passports for £33,000, promising 'trouble free travel' around the world: Belize is closely linked to Britain and hence to the EU.[102] There are countless similar stories.

Migrants may sometimes be admitted officially to countries in which there are demands for cheap labour. During the 1990s thousands of workers were flown from Third World countries direct to European states to work in the North Sea oilfields. In 1999 Danish and British companies were employing Mauritian labourers at 81 pence an hour—said by the TUC to be the lowest wages in Britain.[103] States may also turn a blind eye to limited entry of 'illegals' in order to relax wage pressures, as in Spain, where one report notes that, despite EU controls, 'cheap, illegal African labour is becoming an ever more common sight'.[104] It is *control* of migration that is important for states and for the EU: the ability to regulate migratory movements and to use the issue of migration instrumentally. This racist policy has specific, often tragic, outcomes. In Germany the collapse of the Stalinist regime in the Democratic Republic in 1989 initially prompted triumphalist predictions about unification, including promises of massive growth of an integrated German economy. These ceased when Europe as a whole was affected by world recession; hundreds of workplaces closed and by 1992 unemployment in the German east had risen to 35 to 40 percent.[105] The fascists soon profited: Turner comments on the 'vacuum of uncertainty and despair in which neo-Nazi skinheads and others could seek out foreign born scapegoats on which to blame the economic crisis'.[106] The German foreign minister nonetheless chose this time to declare that immigration was threatening German democracy.[107] Alarmist statements were appearing regularly in the media, with the issue 'firmly planted in national and European Community political agendas'.[108] Confidence among fascist groups rose accordingly:

during 1992 there was a tenfold increase in reported racist violence across the country.[109] Evans describes one outcome:

> *In June 1992 DVU activists began to agitate in Rostock on the Baltic coast of the former GDR against Romani refugees and guestworkers. Pamphlets distributed by the DVU stigmatised these groups in familiar ways. Romani Gypsies were attacked as non-conformist nomads, part of a general 'Gypsy plague' engaged in the systematic harassment of ordinary citizens; immigrants were portrayed as a 'flood' or 'invasion' whose separate culture was threatening to 'swamp' that of Germany; while African guestworkers from the former GDR were characterised as a health threat, infecting the German nation with AIDS. DVU propaganda went on to urge German citizens to take the 'immigrant problem' into their own hands, and there is little doubt that the DVU played a key role in the large scale anti-foreigner pogrom on 24 August 1992 when a guestworker hostel was burnt down.[110]*

The Rostock pogrom was a particularly chilling incident but did nothing to halt the increasingly overt racism of governments and EU bodies. Across the Union there were attempts to induce the white majority population to police non-white people. In France the government brought forward proposals to oblige householders to report non-citizen 'guests' to the police; in Britain legislation appeared which directed employers to check the immigration status of employees. When hundreds of workers in an east London borough were checked by the Home Office on the basis that they had names of African origin, the local MP accused the government of 'Gestapo tactics of the police state. It's a Nazi style witch hunt'.[111]

Although the intensification of racism is always related to specific circumstances, the EU has played a significant role in generalising hostility towards minorities. This is seen in the case of Ireland, where until the mid-1990s there had been no record of consistent opposition to immigration. In 1992 there were a mere 29 applications for asylum in Ireland; by 1997 the figure had risen to 3,883.[112] A key factor was the impact of Fortress Europe legislation in other EU states which had been favoured destinations for asylum seekers. In 1993 Britain introduced an Asylum Act which resulted in a 400 percent increase in decisions against refugees.[113] Allen comments, 'Clearly a number of refugees who did not wish to spend their time in detention in Britain decided to make their application in Ireland instead'.[114] The Irish government introduced a Refugee Act. This was a relatively liberal law by EU standards but, as Ireland was obliged to operate within the framework of the harmonisation of European migration legislation, it incorporated all the usual restrictions. Most important, Ireland was to deport refugees to any third country through which they had travelled in their search for asylum. As Ireland is the most westerly outpost of the EU, most refugees have to touch down in another EU state first. When later there was a wave of hostility towards refugees, the media and politicians undertook an unprecedented attack on asylum seekers, describing them as 'professional beggars' and 'welfare fraudsters', and as bearing a culture 'not akin to Irish culture'.[115] The EU provisions to exclude third country asylum seekers were duly imposed, followed by a policy of detention and proposals for new draconian immigration legislation. In 1998 the first anti-refugee group in Ireland, the Immigration Control Platform, was established. There was soon a further campaign against Roma asylum seekers from eastern Europe, which alleged that 'racial tensions' in the country were about to boil over.[116]

There is similar evidence from Spain and Portugal. Despite the experience of fascism in both countries, until recently there was no active movement which targeted migrants. A recent sharp rise in racist violence cannot be disconnected from the regime of exclusion introduced by the state as part of efforts by the EU to firm up its 'soft underbelly'. The Spanish and Portuguese governments have fallen into line with policies generated by northern neighbours which had already accommodated to populist pressures from the right. Corkill comments, 'Immigration policy has evolved in parallel with the closer alignment between northern and southern Europe,' producing a 'Fortress Iberia'.[117]

For decades Portugal had a relatively open migration policy, especially in relation to its former colonies in Latin America and Africa, and to seasonal migrants from North Africa. Since the harmonisation of EU migration policies, it has become 'a "gendarme" for the European Union'.[118] The Spanish government has joined the most strident elements in the EU by warning of migrant threats from North Africa, and of heightened conflict between Europe and Islam.[119] It strongly supported the EU's Barcelona Declaration of 1995 and a year later introduced a deadline for registration of 'illegals', threatening mass deportations. Writing in 1996, Corkill expressed anxiety that expectations of the mass of people in Spain and Portugal that the EU would deliver new prosperity were likely to turn to disillusion: 'They may begin to regard their immigrant populations as scapegoats for a wide range of social and economic ills'.[120] In 1998 there was a rise in racist attacks, directed primarily against North Africans.[121] In 1999 gangs organised three nights of attacks on Moroccan workers in Catalonia in the country's first large scale incident of racist violence. Their slogan was 'Moors out'.[122]

Movements from below

Governments routinely lament such incidents. Following the attacks in

Catalonia, an official spokesman declared, 'We must show understanding and make sure these people, who have seen the need to leave their country, feel welcome and have opportunities here'.[123] This from the representative of a state which boasted of having made its colonial enclaves in North Africa 'impassable' to migrants, so inhibiting onward movement into Spain and the EU.[124] Similar sentiments have been expressed in Britain, where the Labour government attempted to rationalise its leading role in the war against Serbia by reference to the suffering of Balkan refugees. The British state has been imprisoning asylum seekers, many originating from this region, at the rate of 10,000 a year.[125] In June 1999 it announced the opening of the country's first asylum seeker jail, to be built in Kent, an area judged 'geographically and physically ideally suited' because of its proximity to Channel ports through which many refugees attempt to enter Britain.[126] The EU too sheds crocodile tears over the plight of refugees, all the while directing member states to comply with every element of the Fortress legislation. In February 1999 its tabloid newspaper in Britain, *EP News* (itself an attempt to induce wider popular identification with the European Parliament) reported 'a deterioration in asylum policy in Europe'.[127] Only weeks later NATO bombers were creating millions of new refugees in Kosovo and in Serbia.

Such hypocrisy is an expression of the aim of national governments and of the EU to use immigration opportunistically. They hope to accommodate pressures from the right; at the same time they attempt to capture support for their military adventures from those who identify with victims of oppression. This is an ideological project. It aims to bind workers in member states to their rulers and to a particular vision of 'union'. It rests upon the capacity to fragment and divide the mass of people, above all to weaken solidarities of the working class. It is for this reason that the search for 'Europeanity' and the drive for exclusion have been defined most sharply at times when the EU project has fallen into crisis—and invariably these crises have been linked with heightened working class struggle.

The EU's progress towards a fortified Europe, and the heavy cost in terms of intensified racism and growth of the right, would present a dismal picture if it were not for the responses of a whole range of movements from below. Anti-racist and anti-fascist movements in several countries have been decisive in slowing or even halting fascist advance. In the 1970s the Anti Nazi League in Britain played a key role in derailing the National Front, a task requiring years of focused activity. In France, where in the 1980s it seemed that the FN might achieve a formidable national presence, young activists overcame the accommodationist politics of parties of the left to challenge Le Pen. Although their movement was fragmented and its activities were sometimes ineffectual, there were massive mobilisations of youth, especially in the mid-1980s when hundreds of thousands of school students demonstrated against racist attacks.[128] The movement reasserted itself in a more militant form in the mid-1990s, with large mobilisations against the FN, even in the fascists' electoral strongholds. A demonstration in Paris in 1997 attracted 100,000 people, setting down a marker against fascism which later developments suggest was critical in weakening the right. A significant feature of this demonstration was the presence of large contingents of anti-fascists from other European countries. Similarly, events in Germany from the early 1990s prompted a strong movement of solidarity with victims of racism. There were huge demonstrations in the wake of the Rostock killings of 1992: Turner comments on the contrast between the 'hideous face' of neo-Nazism, 'protested by thousands of silent, candle bearing demonstrators'.[129] In 1999, following attacks on Moroccan workers in Spain, large demonstrations assembled in the Catalonian town of Terrassa under the slogan, 'We are all neighbours'.[130]

Measures of state racism, in line with EU policies on exclusion, have also prompted movements of opposition. While EU ministers met in Barcelona in 1995, an 'alternative conference' of socialists and anti-racists was held in the city which attacked the hypocrisy of the Union and especially the Islamophobia implicit in the Barcelona Declaration.[131] In Greece measures to close the country's 'permeable' borders to refugees were criticised on the left as xenophobic and 'drafted to please Brussels'.[132] Such solidarity, built from below, is likely to become more important. There is every sign that European economies and the EU itself are going to pass through further crises. A key issue will be a contraction of state spending in Germany, where in June 1999 major budget cuts were announced. The German government also declared its intention to reduce sharply the country's contribution to EU finances, currently about two thirds of the total.[133] These difficulties must be added to continuing problems over the euro and EU monetary policy, with its pressures on spending in every member country.

These developments take place at a time when inequalities across Europe are becoming far more marked. By 1995, 53 million people in the Union were impoverished (receiving half average per capita income)—a 40 percent increase since 1975.[134] Wealth in the EU is now concentrated in a long narrow strip of territory stretching from London, through Belgium, Frankfurt, Munich, and northern Italy up to Paris, and called 'the blue banana' by Eurocrats.[135] This zone is home to the very rich; it also contains many of the most poor, notably in London and in the Paris region. In Belgium per capita income of the old mining area of Hainault is less than half that of neighbouring Brussels.[136] There are further concentrations of poor people in regions with large rural populations—in Portugal, Spain, southern Italy and Greece—but very large numbers are in decaying industrial centres in Britain and in eastern Germany, where the poor are now poorer than peasants of the Mediterranean zones.[137] Further pressure from governments intent on reducing state spending is likely to increase volatility, stimulating resistance, workers' struggles—and other reactions, including interventions from the right.

Some Euro-politicians have already warned of the need to secure the EU against new 'global threats'. According to Tom Spencer, Tory leader of the Security and Defence Policy Committee of the European Parliament, Europe faces immense pressures from the Third World. He warns that economic crisis, population growth and political collapse are likely to drive northwards tens of millions of desperate people: 'the wretched of the earth'.[138] Europe requires a more coherent policy to deal with this inundantation, argues Spencer, and to quell 'the genuine fears and perceptions of our citizens'. Urgent action is needed before 'civilisation' [ie Western Europe] is submerged by this 'tide of misery'.[139] There has also been increased concern about refugees from neighbouring regions, those described by Blair as on 'on the doorstep of Europe'. Before the EU briefly admitted Kosovan refugees during the war against Serbia, there was a sustained campaign of deportation of Bosnians and many Albanians were refused entry. The German government told the EU that its doors were 'closed' to such asylum-seekers. Turning once more to the slogans of the extreme right, foreign minister Klaus Kinkel declared, 'Our boat is practically full'.[140] It seems certain that events will follow a well worn path, with resistance from below prompting governments and Eurocrats to accommodate the populists and to reach for the racist card.

Internationalism

The record shows that decisive struggles against nationalism and nation-like ideologies such as Europeanism are those mobilised from below. This is clear from the most recent events, including the mobilisations against racism. Turner notes the contribution of the defiance of workers to the anti-racist movement in Germany. Turner comments that in 1993, despite mass unemployment, closures and general insecurity, the mass strikes of workers in the east played a key role.[141] They were largely successful, part of a movement across the country which maintained collective confidence, 'acting in this way as a barrier to the rise of an extremist right in both eastern and western Germany in a potentially dangerous period of turbulence'.[142] There was a similar experience in France, when at a period in the mid-1990s the FN was on the rise, opposition to government cuts and proposals for privatisation produced a sustained mass strike movement of enormous power. Millions participated in workplace actions and in demonstrations which stimulated renewed confidence within the working class. The effect was to increase collective confidence in general, helping to prompt widespread solidarity with *sans papiers*—'illegals'—and demonstrations against racist laws. Fysh and Wolfreys comment that, despite the FN's earlier surge, 'after the strike movement of December 1995 had severely dented the government's self confidence, by the end of 1996, the initiative was passing decisively to the left, thanks to a revival of militant anti-racism'.[143]

Sustained mass struggles emphasise the real class character of the EU. In 1997 the European Commission threatened action against strikers in France for preventing a free movement of goods across the single European market. Later the European Court of Justice ruled that the French government had failed to act decisively against the strikes and warned that member states must move effectively against 'perpetrators' of disruptive action.[144] Solidarity, especially active solidarity across national borders, will become more important. There are already precedents, such as the demonstration in 1997 of 50,000 people from across Europe who converged on an EU summit in Amsterdam to protest against Europe wide unemployment. In the same year car plants in seven countries were closed by a strike in solidarity with sacked Renault workers in Belgium. Demonstrators from many countries and a host of companies then protested at Renault HQ in Paris denouncing 'sweatshop Europe'—an exemplary action which caused alarm in corporate boardrooms and in European capitals. These mobilisations were notable for their multicultural character, bringing together workers of many origins, notably those officially placed outside 'European culture'. Reporting on these events, *The Guardian* commented that 'the Euro-demo is born'.[145] Here is a glimpse of internationalism, of a movement from below which can emerge from what Luxemburg called 'the capacity for action and the revolutionary will of the international proletariat'.

Notes

Thanks to John Rees, Judy Cox, Adrian Budd and Ronny Geller for their comments on this article in draft

1   *The Guardian*, 26 March 1999.
2   *The Observer*, 7 January 1996.
3   In 1957 signatories to the Treaty of Rome, which established the European Economic Community (EEC), agreed to 'establish the foundations of an ever closer union among the European peoples'.
4   G Strange, 'The Role of Economic Policy in the Europeanisation of the TUC', *Contemporary Politics*, vol 1, no 4 (1995), p42.

5   V Fonskos, 'The Italien Left and the enlargement of the European Union',
    Contemporary Politics, vol 3, no 2 (1997), p135.
6   *The Guardian*, 13 January 1999.
7   *The Independent*, 27 May 1997.
8   *The Guardian*, 4 August 1997.
9   K Marx and F Engels, *Collected Works*, vol 6 (London, 1980), p495.
10 Ibid, p497.
11 Their attitude to the nation state was modified only to the extent that they
    endorsed struggle for 'national independence', when masses of people asserted the
    right of independence of nations from colonising powers.
12 P Nettl, *Rosa Luxemburg* (Oxford, 1969), p393.
13 C Shore, 'Imagining the New Europe: Identity and Heritage in European
    Community Discourse', in P Graves-Brown et al (eds), *The Anthropology of
    Europe: Identity and Boundaries in Conflict* (Oxford, 1996), pp102-103.
14 M Lowy, *Fatherland or Mother Earth?* (London, 1998), p70.
15 Attali is former head of the European Bank for Reconstruction and Development.
    Quoted in A Burgess, *Divided Europe* (London, 1997), p60.
16 E Gellner, 'Nationalism and Politics in Eastern Europe', *New Left Review* 189
    (1991), p131.
17 D Kenrick, 'Selective Memory', *Jewish Socialist* 39 (1998), p12.
18 Ibid, p13. Human Rights Watch has reported 'blatant discrimination and violent
    crimes' against Roma communities in the Czech Republic and Slovakia (see *The
    Independent*, 21 October 1997). There have been repeated murders of Roma and
    systematic attacks, described as 'pogroms', in the Czech Republic, Hungary and
    Bulgaria. For an account of the predicament of Roma in Eastern Europe see
    Refugee Council, *Unwanted Journey* (London, 1999).
19 D Kenrick, op cit, p13.
20 From articles published in newspapers in south east England, quoted in *The
    Independent*, 17 November 1998.
21 Refugee Council, op cit, p67.
22 Ibid, p72.
23 *The Guardian*, 7 August 1998.
24 Ibid.
25 M Lowy, op cit, p70.
26 'The Common Market', *International Socialism* 77 (old series), p7.
27 A Milward, *The European Rescue of the Nation State* (London, 1994).
28 A Callinicos, 'Europe: the Mounting Crisis', *International Socialism* 75 (1997),
    p25.
29 P Rietbergen, *Europe: A Cultural History* (London, 1998), pxvii.
30 G Delanty, *Inventing Europe* (Basingstoke, 1995), p71.
31 Quoted in O Waever and M Kelstrup, 'Europe and its Nations: Political and
    Cultural Identities', in O Waever, B Buzan, M Kelstrup and P Lemaitre, *Identity,
    Migration and the New Security Agenda in Europe* (London, 1993), p65.
32 G Delanty, op cit, p71.
33 Such attitudes were conceived within the European bourgeoisies, or among
    intellectuals who were influenced by changes brought by capitalism. Elsewhere
    'Europe' was viewed differently: in the Middle East and North Africa, for
    example, the *franj* ('French'—a synonym for Europeans) were widely held to be
    violent and unsophisticated.
34 For analyses of variations on the 'Europe'/'Europeans' theme, see G Delanty, op
    cit; P Rietbergen, op cit; T Patterson, *Inventing Western Civilization* (New York,
    1997); and S Federici (ed), *Enduring Western Civilization* (Westport, 1995).
35 G Delanty, op cit, p112.
36 G Kolko, *The Politics of War* (London, 1969), p361.

37   'The Common Market', *International Socialism* 77 (old series), p9.
38   G Robinson, writing in 1949 in the US State Department's 'house journal', *Foreign Affairs*, quoted in Burgess, op cit, p146.
39   Ibid.
40   G Delanty, op cit, p121. This comment points up the extent to which the US actively intervened in Europe in both material and ideological senses, though it risks understating the extent to which European ruling classes were engaged alongside American capitalism in attempting to shape the post-war order.
41   B Connolly, *The Rotten Heart of Europe* (London, 1995), pix.
42   Britain's imperial past had left a pattern of overseas investments and strategic interests which caused some sections of capital to oppose further engagement in Europe. In 1957 the British bosses' organisation, the CBI, declared against the EEC, because 'this would mean for the UK the end of the imperial preference system' (Quoted in 'The Common Market', *International Socialism* 77 (old series), p10. See also A Callinicos, op cit.
43   M Martiniello, 'Citizenship of the European Union: A Critical View', in R Baubock (ed), *From Aliens to Citizens: Redefining the Status of Immigrants in Europe* (Aldershot, 1994) p33.
44   B Connolly, op cit, Preface.
45   Ibid, p33.
46   O Waever and M Kelstrup, op cit, pp65-66.
47   Ibid, p65.
48   M Martiniello, op cit, p40.
49   O Waever and M Kelstrup, op cit, p66.
50   Quoted in M Martiniello, op cit, p40.
51   Ibid.
52   R Cohen and D Joly, *Reluctant Hosts: Europe and its Refugees* (Aldershot, 1989), p15.
53   M Martiniello, op cit, p33.
54   Had the British NF not been defeated by anti-fascist mobilisations in the 1970s, Britain too would surely have seen a further revival of the right.
55   C Bambery, 'Euro-fascism: The Lessons of the Past and Current Tasks', *International Socialism* 60 (1993), p57.
56   Ibid.
57   M Evans, 'Languages of Racism within Contemporary Europe', in B Jenkins and S Sofos, *Nation and Identity in Contemporary Europe* (London, 1996), pp47-48.
58   C Bambery, op cit, p57.
59   M Evans, op cit, p49.
60   Ibid, p47.
61   Ibid, p48.
62   Ibid.
63   P Fysh and J Wolfreys, *The Politics of Racism in France* (London, 1998), p45.
64   Ibid.
65   Ibid.
66   Ibid, p44.
67   C W de Wenden, 'North African Immigration and the French Political Imaginary', in M Silverman (ed), *Race, Discourse and Power in France* (Aldershot, 1991), p100.
68   M Evans, op cit, p47.
69   P Fysh and J Wolfreys, op cit, p111. See these authors' account of changes in the ideology of fascism in France during the 1970s and 1980s, ch 5.
70   M Evans, op cit, p49.
71   C Grant, *Inside the House that Jacques Built* (London, 1994), p223.

72   Minority Rights Group, *Refugees in Europe: The Hostile New Agenda* (London, 1997), p22.
73   S Castles and M Miller, *The Age of Migration* (London, 1993), p127.
74   Quoted in A Burgess, op cit, p57.
75   Ibid.
76   Ibid, p58.
77   A Callinicos, op cit, p31.
78   See, among numerous publications, Waever et al, op cit, ch 4; S Garcia (ed), *European Identity and the Search for Legitimacy* (London, 1993); M Gabel and H Palmer, 'Understanding Variation in Public Support for European integration', *European Journal of Political Research*, 27 (1995).
79   S Panebianco, 'European Citizenship and European Identity: from the Treaty of Maastricht to Public Opinion Attitudes', *Jean Monnet Working Papers in Comparative and International Politics* (University of Catania, 1996).
80   D Joly, *Haven or Hell, Asylum Policies and Refugees in Europe* (London, 1996), p82.
81   S Collinson, *Shore to Shore: The Politics of Migration in Euro-Maghreb Relations* (London, 1996), p40.
82   M Lister, *The European Union and the South* (London, 1997), p101.
83   Ibid.
84   Ibid. Lister notes that there was ample evidence available to show that human fertility rates in North Africa had in fact declined sharply.
85   *The Guardian*, 16 November 1991.
86   S Collinson, op cit, p19.
87   Minority Rights Group, op cit, p13.
88   E Said, *Orientalism* (London, 1978).
89   S Huntington, 'The Clash of Civilizations?', *Foreign Affairs* (Summer 1993).
90   Quoted in M Salla, 'Political Islam in the West', *Third World Quarterly,* vol 18, no 4 (1997), p733.
91   The Runnymede Trust, *Islamophobia* (London, 1997). p9.
92   P Fysh and J Wolfreys, op cit, p185.
93   T Bjorgo, '"The Invaders", "The Traitors" and "The Resistance Movement": The Extreme Right's Conceptualisation of Opponents and Self in Scandinavia', in T Modood and P Werbner, *The Politics of Multicultualism in the New Europe* (London, 1997), p67.
94   *The Spectator*, 19 October 1991, quoted in The Runnymede Trust, op cit.
95   M Evans, op cit, p49.
96   See The Runnymede Trust, op cit, p9.
97   *New Internationalist*, April 1999, p5.
98   *The Guardian*, 4 November 1997.
99   *The Guardian*, 28 July 1998.
100   *The Guardian*, 29 June 1998. Elsewhere in Europe, refugee protests at such centres had become almost routine. Repeated riots at the Campsfield centre in southern England went almost unrecorded, despite warnings that the prison had become a 'powder keg'.
101   R Miles, *Racism After Race Relations* (London, 1991), p18.
102   *The Guardian,* 21 July 1999; *The Independent,* 21 July 1999.
103   *The Observer,* 7 February 1999.
104   *The Guardian*, 29 August 1998. In 1997 Spain was admitting up to 5,000 workers a year. *Financial Times,* 30 August 1997
105   L Turner, *Fighting for Partnership: Labor and Politics in a Unified Germany* (Ithaca, 1998), p44.
106   Ibid.
107   B Buzan and B A Roberson, in O Waever et al, op cit, p132.

108   Ibid, p131.
109   Ibid.
110   M Evans, op cit, p48.
111   Brian Sedgemore, Labour MP for Hackney South, speaking after 600 workers with 'African' names working for Hackney council were checked by the Home Office. *The Observer*, 25 June 1995.
112   K Allen, 'Immigration and the Celtic Tiger: A Land of a Thousand Welcomes', in G Dale and M Cole, *The European Union and Migrant Labour* (Oxford, 1999), p117.
113   Ibid.
114   Ibid.
115   This was associated, argues Allen, with the greatly increased inequality and sense of relative deprivation which accompanied the boom of the 'Celtic Tiger' economy. Ibid, pp123-127.
116   *The Guardian*, 5 August 1998.
117   D Corkill, 'Multiple National Identities, Immigration and Racism in Spain and Portugal', in B Jenkins and S Sofos, op cit, pp164-165.
118   Ibid.
119   Spanish foreign minister Javier Solana, *The Independent*, 8 February 1995.
120   D Corkill, op cit, p169.
121   *The Guardian*, 29 August 1998.
122   *The Guardian*, 17 July 1999; *The Independent*, 21 July 1999.
123   Josep Pique in *The Guardian*, 17 July 1999.
124   *The Guardian,* 29 August 1998.
125   *The Independent*, 28 June 1999.
126   Ibid.
127   *EP News*, January/February 1999.
128   P Fysh and J Wolfreys, op cit, ch 6.
129   L Turner, op cit, p133.
130   *The Guardian*, 17 July 1999.
131   *The Guardian*, 28 November 1995.
132   *The Guardian*, 27 November 1996.
133   *The Guardian*, 21 July 1999.
134   L Leontidou and A Afouxenidis, 'Boundaries of Social Exclusion in Europe', in R Hudson and A Williams (eds), *Divided Europe* (London, 1999), p259.
135   *The Independent*, 14 August 1998.
136   Quoted in M Haynes, 'European Union and its Periphery: Inclusion and Exclusion', *Economic and Political Weekly*, 29 August 1998, p87.
137   Report of the Urban Task Force in *The Observer*, 27 June 1999.
138   *The Independent*, 11 June 1997.
139   Ibid.
140   *The Guardian*, 20 March 1997.
141   L Turner, op cit, p139.
142   Ibid.
143   P Fysh and J Wolfreys, op cit, p201.
144   *The Guardian*, 5 November and 10 December 1997.
145   *The Guardian*, 12 March 1997.

The return of Italian Communism?

TOM BEHAN

Ten years after the collapse of Stalinism there appears to be some degree of resurgence of the old Communist parties. In Spain and France, under different guises, names and faces, the old parties are reappearing. In Italy an organisation that calls itself Rifondazione Comunista (Communist Refoundation), claiming over 100,000 members, won 8.6 percent of the vote in the 1996 national elections and slightly more in local council elections in 1997. Its small parliamentary group was instrumental in keeping Romano Prodi's Olive Tree coalition in power through 1997 and 1998. Mike Gonzalez of *International Socialism* asked Tom Behan to explore the recent history of the left in Italy to find an explanation for this apparent paradox and to try to assess how it will affect the rebuilding of an authentic revolutionary socialist tradition in Italy.

IS: What were the immediate effects of the end of Stalinism in Italy?

TB: After the fall of the Berlin Wall the leadership of the Italian Communist Party (PCI), an organisation which still had around 1 million members, moved quickly to assess the impact, both political and practical, of the fall of the Berlin Wall. Through the 1980s the PCI had moved to the right, endorsing anti-strike laws, and supporting Italy's decision to remain within NATO in 1986. Its base in the working class was shrinking and it was coming under increasing attack by the Socialist Party. It became more and more reluctant to defend its association with

Eastern European Communism. In 1989 the party's general secretary, Achille Occhetto, immediately announced an emergency conference at which the PCI would dissolve and be replaced by a new formation. What form the new organisation would take was unclear—so it became known as *la cosa*, 'the thing'. The thing in question was to rename the party and completely rewrite its underlying programme.

IS: What was the effect of all this confusion on the PCI membership?

TB: Tremendous disorientation. Many people left, though a lot of young people actually joined in this period because they were enthused by the whole debate about communism, appalled by the attacks of the Socialists, and felt some undefined responsibility to defend the heritage of communism. There were others who had become local government officials in quite powerful positions through PCI membership and they were quick to jump ship. It was certainly a time of intense debate. The PCI leadership argued that the problem was that the party had been slow to understand the failures of Stalinism and that now they must be publicly condemned so that the new 'thing' could go on to become a party of government. On the other hand, there was an important layer of rank and file members, of activists, who argued against this essentially social democratic line. When the conference convened in February 1991, it split messily in two; the bureaucrats joined the PDS (Party of the Democratic Left) while a significant minority of activists and many from the Stalinist left joined Rifondazione.

IS: This split must have reflected a division that already existed, at least in potential, within the PCI. What are the political origins of this conflict—which presumably was carried into the new organisations emerging from the split?

TB: The first thing that happened after the announcement of the split was a messy and drawn out battle over who owned the traditional symbols of the party—in fact they went to court over it! When the 'thing' was finally unveiled on the last day of the conference, it turned out to be the PDS whose banner carried an oak tree at the top, symbolising peace and harmony, but also a much smaller hammer and sickle at the bottom. Rifondazione claimed the hammer and sickle for itself—but as things turned out the PDS soon dropped the symbol and Rifondazione took it back anyway.

You have to go back to 1921 to understand all this. The Italian Communist Party (PCI) was born in 1921, in a revolutionary period. It was still the time of the revolutionary upsurge of the working class after the First World War, the *biennio rosso* (the red two years), when the Russian Revolution still enjoyed a massive political influence. That was reflected in the authentically revolutionary character of the early PCI under Gramsci's leadership. But in October 1922 Mussolini came to power; for a year or two the PCI managed to maintain some kind of public existence until it was driven completely underground by 1924-1925. It remained a clandestine party for the next 20 years. Its leaders left Italy to escape fascist repression, leaving a courageous but dwindling internal membership behind working in conditions of the most absolute secrecy.

Abroad the PCI leadership toed the Moscow line and adopted Stalinist postures. But that transformation occurred largely without the knowledge of an internal membership which had no access to the PCI's new publications which praised Stalin and renounced the revolutionary politics of its early years, and therefore probably did not know that the party of Gramsci was dead. But it is these people who became the guiding force of the resistance movement that was beginning to emerge on a national scale in 1943. The PCI's membership grew to around 5,000 to 6,000 after a series of successful strikes in March 1943. By February 1945 the trickle had grown into a stream and membership reached 90,000.

The PCI leaders clearly saw that, on the one hand, they had no means of controlling this movement from the outside, and on the other that the resistance could be transformed into a new mass Communist party after the war. Under these circumstances they had no alternative but to give the leaders of the mass movement their head—though they tried with limited success to Stalinise them at the same time.

By 1945 the leadership came to define what they called the 'two track approach', in which the leadership clearly pursue a parliamentary road while hinting to their own rank and file that this is merely a Trojan horse and that when the day comes they will build the barricades and get rid of all these bastards with whom they are currently sharing the parliamentary benches. The call for all weapons to be handed in to the authorities by April 1945 produced a limited response; it was clear that many workers and resistance fighters were keeping them for the insurrection to come. Luigi Longo, the party's deputy leader, complained that the membership was suffering from 'the machine gun disease', as exemplified by the two day armed occupation of the Milan Prefecture in November 1947 under the leadership of PCI Central Committee member Giancarlo Pajetta.

Then, in 1948, the party leader and exemplary Stalinist Palmiro Togliatti was shot and almost killed outside parliament. Within 24 hours, with no instructions from the leadership, the guns that had been kept oiled and ready for three years came out and most of the northern cities found themselves under the control of the PCI. This insurrectionary atmosphere within the PCI led to considerable anxiety in the deepening Cold War atmosphere and the CIA organised a 'Gladio' or 'stay behind' army that would act in the event of a Communist rising. In response the PCI itself maintained a clandestine organisation and safe houses and escape routes. But the PCI leaders had already embarked on the 'long march' along the parliamentary road, and no voice was raised against them within the Party. The PCI's 2 million members fell in behind the leadership; the 'class of the Resistance' provided the loyal backbone of the party through the 1950s and 1960s. The newer supporters were wedded to a parliamentary perspective and had little sympathy for direct struggle. In Turin, for example, sales of the PCI daily *L'Unità* fell consistently through the 1960s, even though party membership in the city stood at around 20,000 and electoral support ran at about 40 percent.

There were still arms held in factories by the older generation; arms dumps were still being found when they knocked old factories down to build flats—they'd come across 30 mortars and 500 machine guns in working order in the basement. But the bulk of arms had been surrendered after the events of 1948.

***IS*: A new generation of young worker and student activists emerged in Italy, as it did elsewhere in Europe, in 1968. Did they turn to the PCI?**

TB: No, the PCI began to suffer in 1968 with the growth of an alternative movement and the new organisations of the revolutionary left like Lotta Continua, Avanguardia Operaia and the rest. These organisations exploded between 1968 and 1972. But they entered a long crisis with an industrial downturn in 1972-1973 and by 1976 they were all effectively dead. We are talking here about organisations with tens of thousands of activists, six MPs, six radio stations and about three national newspapers. Yet by 1976 the radio stations were closed down, there were no MPs left and the great mass demonstrations were winding down in the face of state repression. From the late 1970s a new organisation, Democrazia Proletaria, tried to gather together the fragments into what amounted to a new centrist organisation. It embraced peace campaigners, environmentalists and Left Catholics in a kind of 'container party' which disintegrated under the weight of its own contradictions in 1989. At that point nearly half the organisation left to join the Greens, including their parliamentary representatives who took with them the state subsidy which had made up 95 percent of the organisation's finances. Those who were left eventually joined Rifondazione.

IS: **How did the PCI react to the political crisis of the early 1970s?**

TB: The real turning point was 1973 when the PCI declared the 'historic compromise'. Its reasons were economic and political. The rise in the price of oil had a dramatic impact on Italy, and in the face of the crisis the Christian Democrats turned to the PCI for support in exchange for a promise that if they behaved as a responsible national party they might one day become part of government. It was what the leadership had been waiting for. They seized the opportunity, arguing that workers would have to accept cuts in their living standards as the price for becoming a party of government—an argument they seemed to win with some of their own rank and file.

At the same time a vicious argument broke out within the party over the implications of the overthrow of Allende in Chile in September 1973. For the left of the party, the 'two track approach' that the PCI had pursued since the end of the war was no longer tenable in the face of what happened in Chile. The party's general secretary, Enrico Berlinguer, replied in a series of articles in November, arguing (a) that Allende had tried to go too quickly and alienated the right wing, and (b) that 51 percent of the vote would not be enough to govern—you could only do that with the support of the right. That was the historic compromise.

The timing of the debate was also affected by the rise of left wing terrorism through 1973. The emergence of the left wing terrorist groups was a symptom of the failure of the 1968 movement. At first, workers did not look unfavourably at the kidnapping or even kneecapping of factory managers and the wall posters in which the hostages confessed their involvement in an exploitative system. By the mid-1970s you still had mass demonstrations of 200,000 to 300,000—but they often ended up in shootouts, when the armed groups would suddenly leap out of the crowd and start firing at the police, who would fire back. By the end of the decade the demonstrations had virtually stopped and the state seized the opportunity to criminalise left wing activity under the guise of anti-terrorist laws. The effect was to drive the PCI further to the right. They did not oppose new laws which allowed preventative custody of up to 11 years simply on the basis of an unproven accusation.

IS: **That's the background to the rise of Rifondazione. Can we look at how it developed after 1991?**

TB: In a sense Rifondazione carries within it the same contradictions as its predecessor. It contains on the one hand the parliamentarians who are conducting a bourgeois battle, and on the other hand local branches that have weekly meetings on Che Guevara or the environment, who invite local stewards to speak, who confront the police, throw petrol bombs and support radical struggles around the world. The 100,000 who joined Rifondazione during its first year were the activists on the one hand, and the more unreconstructed Stalinists on the other, as well as the minority of activists from Democrazia Proletaria. The vast majority of inactive PCI members joined the PDS.

IS: **Italian politics through most of the 1990s seem highly volatile— yet they also brought the masses back onto the streets, particularly during the Berlusconi presidency. How did that affect the refounding of Communism?**

TB: One of the constants of Italian electoral politics is electoral instability with sometimes up to five parties involved in national government. In 1992 the so called 'Tangentopoli' bribery scandals began to break. In less than two years five ministers were forced to resign for corruption, the Socialist Party fell apart and the Christian Democrats split. Into this atmosphere of extreme instability stepped the unpredictable right wing multi-millionaire media magnate Silvio Berlusconi. He won the 1994 elections and immediately brought the neo-fascist MSI (Italian Social Movement) into the government. Meanwhile the country seemed obsessed by an unprecedented series of scandals acted out nightly on television, as minister after minister was subjected to televised interrogations by examining magistrates.

At the same time there was an enormous fear of this new government which in a sense served to rejuvenate the left, and particularly Rifondazione. Up till this moment neither the PDS nor Rifondazione seemed capable of organising themselves or of leading anything. Symptomatic was the fact that neither had prepared for the national demonstration of 25th April, held annually to commemorate the liberation from fascism. In previous years it had attracted around 5,000 people, but it took on a different significance when Berlusconi invited the fascists into government. It was left to *Il Manifesto*, a socialist paper selling some 30,000 copies daily, to call for a mass demonstration. Some 300,000 turned up to march through Milan in the pouring rain.

It was a key moment in the rebuilding of the left. Berlusconi ignored it and contrived to get his friends, who had been involved in bribery, out of jail. But as they left they were met with angry demonstrations and pelted with coins. And when Berlusconi then turned his attack against Italy's state pension scheme, one of the most progressive in Europe in 1994, the unions were forced to call a month long series of protest demonstrations in defence of pensions and the welfare state. But whenever the union bureaucrats tried to speak from behind huge plate glass screens, they were pelted with bottles, tomatoes, nuts and bolts. This response recalled the activities of the *autonomisti* in the late 1970s. The crowd was there to support the pensions scheme and the welfare system against Berlusconi, but they were also there to protest against the shoddy deals their leaders had been making through the previous years. Not everyone was throwing missiles of course—but around 30 percent of the crowd were usually involved and the rest weren't protesting. Realizing this, Rifondazione began to try to build on that mood and move with it.

Rifondazione presented candidates for the 1996 elections with a thoroughgoing ten point reformist programme. It held a series of mass rallies and public meetings and the sales of its newspaper *Liberazione* almost doubled. It seemed that Rifondazione was rediscovering the so called 'two track' approach of the past, presenting itself as a party of government on the one hand and as the leadership of the rank and file struggles on the other. The 1990s had seen a rapid growth of rank and file workplace organisation, building on the *cobas*, or base committees, that had first grown up in the public sector in the 1980s. The old PCI transmission belt was no longer functioning and the influence of the national trade union federations slowly fragmenting. In the spring of 1999 these organisations could call local strikes against the war in Kosovo in many Italian cities.

By 1997 Rifondazione was increasing its trade union vote; on the other hand, while it could hardly lay claim to being a party of government with just over 8 percent of the vote, it did hold the balance of power in parliament. Its support kept in power an Olive Tree centre-left coalition committed to cuts and privatisation. Increasingly the refounded Communists were splitting along familiar lines. Their leader Cossutta, an old hardline Stalinist who joined Rifondazione because the PDS didn't make him a good enough offer, began to press for 'programmatic agreements' with the PDS and a 'dented shield' policy, familiar to British socialists, in relation to Prodi and his Olive Tree government. On the other hand, a wing of the party led by Bertinotti held to a more contradictory position of various factions seeking to work with the mass movement. Eventually Rifondazione split in October 1998 and Cossutta joined the government.

There's no doubt that today it is the most significant organisation within the mass struggle. But it hasn't yet resolved its relationship with its own origins. It has not analysed Russia or Cuba, because it would mean more splits and have electoral repercussions. So it constantly sidesteps the need to rediscover the authentic revolutionary socialist tradition. It can't decide whether it wants to be married to capitalism or divorced from it—or occupy separate rooms in the same house. There are now no models of 'actually existing socialism' for it to hide behind other than Cuba. While there has been a continuity of organisation in Italy, it remains fragmented and disorganised. The combination of a political vacuum and a militant and increasingly active working class is an exciting propect for socialists. But it can only develop a political direction when its leadership breaks decisively with a past in which it has always been wedded to parliamentary democracy and the promise of reform, while the rank and file struggled to deliver a blow against capitalism itself.

Freedom fighters or Comintern army? The International Brigades in Spain

ANDY DURGAN

By 1936, in a world ravaged by economic crisis and mass unemployment, after the victories of Mussolini and Hitler and the emergence of similar movements elsewhere, fascism seemed unstoppable. But the 1930s also saw the rise of huge working class resistance, of mass strikes, militant anti-fascism and political radicalisation. When the Spanish Civil War began it immediately became a rallying point for millions who saw that there was, at last, a chance to stop the fascist beast in its tracks. Only in this context can we understand why nearly 30,000 men from 53 different countries were prepared to go and fight and, in many cases, die in Spain in one of the most dramatic examples of internationalism in working class history. The impact of the Spanish war has been such that it has generated more literature than any other war—over 40,000 titles according to one estimate[1]—as well as having inspired a generation of poets, writers and artists. As volunteer Walter Gregory recalled many years later no 'other international or domestic political issue [had] such an explosive impact upon the British working class'.[2]

When the International Brigades were given an emotional and multitudinous farewell in Barcelona on 28 October 1938, the Communist leader Dolores Ibárruri, 'La Pasionaria', declared, 'You can go proudly. You are history. You are legend…the heroic example of democracy's solidarity and universality.' Like all legends, that of the International Brigades wavers between myth and reality. The opening of the former Soviet archives means that we can now get an even clearer view of the nature and role of the Brigades. Thousands of working class militants showed with their heroism and sacrifice what proletarian internationalism could really mean. But their participation was also part of a wider policy engineered by Stalin both to win an alliance with the Western democracies and to maintain his influence in the international labour movement. The International Brigades, like the rest of the Communist movement, were subordinated to this aim.

From the start the war in Spain became the centre of international attention. There was much at stake: the balance of power between the democracies and the emerging authoritarian regimes, the danger of the war spreading beyond Spain's frontiers, and the spectre of revolution. It was the fascist powers which reacted first, seeing in Franco a valuable ally and in Spain a theatre of operations to try out new weapons and strategies. The majority of foreigners who took part in the civil war did so on the fascist side. The Italians sent at least 70,000 men during the nearly three years that the war lasted, the Germans 14,000, mainly advisers, artillery and airmen, the Portuguese dictatorship 20,000, and there were 34,000 Foreign Legion and Moroccan troops. This manpower was accompanied by abundant supplies of arms, ammunition and aircraft. There were few genuine fascist volunteers, nearly all being regular army personnel. The largest volunteer force was the 600 raised by the Irish fascist leader Eoin O'Duffy, whose only contribution of note was to open fire on their own side.

The bourgeois democracies, led by Britain, France and the USA, balked at being drawn into a war that could undermine their attempts to maintain peace in Europe. The revolution taking place in much of the Republican zone in 1936 made them even more reluctant to back a government that seemed to have little control over the situation and, when it did manage to exert control, was under the increasing dominance of the Communist Party. The desperate attempts by the Communists and their allies to present the civil war as a simple defence of democracy was never going to convince the Western governments, or at least these countries' ruling classes, whose natural sympathies lay with Franco. Although the French Popular Front government was initially prepared to send military supplies to its Spanish counterparts, it was soon persuaded by the British Tory administration that helping the Republic would damage imperial interests in the Mediterranean. Hence these powers' backing for the cynical policy of non-intervention. Germany and Italy also adhered to the Non-Intervention Committee, and then systematically ignored its decisions. The effect of non-intervention, which was only ever seriously pursued by the democracies, was to deny the Republic desperately needed military aid and facilitate the fascist victory.

The organisation of the International Brigades

Prior to the establishment of the International Brigades there were already hundreds of foreign volunteers fighting in the workers' militias. These included political refugees already living in Spain and individuals who made their way into Spain once the war started. Most of these foreigners joined up in Barcelona where up to 1,500 international volunteers attached themselves, sometimes quite arbitrarily, to the anarchist, Communist and POUM militias in the first weeks of the war.[3] They included over 200 athletes who had come to the Catalan capital to take part in the People's Olympiad, which was to have been the left's answer to the Nazi organised official games in Germany.

The arrival of large numbers of foreign volunteers in the Republican zone would not start until after the Comintern's decision to form the Brigades. Neither the anarchists nor the independent Marxist groups had the strength outside Spain to organise a force of any significance and the Socialist and Labour parties lacked the political willpower to do so. At first the Soviet government opposed even sending money and medical aid because it feared this would be used by Germany and Italy to justify helping the fascist side. Instead it had immediately started to organise non-military aid both through the Comintern and the Soviet trade unions. On 23 August, Stalin's government accepted the French proposal for the setting up of a Non-Intervention Committee, 'on condition that the USSR was not responsible for Comintern actions, that Germany and Italy must cease aid to Franco and that Portugal must accept non-intervention'.[4]

The Soviet Union decided to support the Republic militarily once it became clear that the scale of fascist intervention could tip the balance of forces decisively in favour of Franco. Soviet military aid did not come, however, without conditions. The whole Spanish gold reserve was shipped to the USSR for 'safekeeping' before any arms arrived on Spanish soil and subsequently the Republic was grossly overcharged for the arms sent.[5] During the following two years the USSR sent some 2,000 military advisers and airmen along with military aid that would prove crucial in holding up Franco's advance. However, along with this aid came the Soviet secret police, the NKVD, and Stalin's demand for an end to the revolution. Underlining these conditions was Stalin's aim to keep the civil war going until an alliance was formed with the democracies to face the inevitable war in Europe.

The decision to form the International Brigades was taken at the Comintern Executive Committee meeting of 18 September 1936, only nine days after the first meeting of the Non-Intervention Committee, and should be seen within the context of the Soviet commitment to send military aid to the Republic.[6] The setting up of such a force had several advantages for the USSR. It would be a very clear indication throughout the world of Soviet internationalism and anti-fascism and thus reinforce Communist influence. In particular, the organising of the Brigades on a non-sectarian basis, where not just Communists but socialists, independents and even liberals would be recruited, fitted perfectly with the politics of the Popular Front. The creation of the Brigades would also solve the problem of what to do with Communist émigrés living in the USSR and proved a very convenient way of introducing NKVD agents into Spain.

The actual organising of the International Brigades was to be carried out by the Communist parties, each being given a quota of volunteers to recruit. A key role was reserved for the French Communist Party (PCF) in getting the volunteers into Spain, and various Comintern leaders went to France to help with this operation. In Spain itself Albacete was chosen as the Intertnational Brigades' base and the first volunteers arrived there on 13 October, two days before the first Soviet arms ship docked in Cartagena. They were soon joined by other foreigners already fighting in Spain. On 22 October the Republican government officially recognised the International Brigades as part of the Republican Army, albeit with their own commanders and infrastructure.

The composition of the Brigades

Despite the official Communist position that the International Brigades would be a military extension of the Popular Front, the reality was that they were heavily dependent on the Communists. Between 80 and 90 percent of the Germans, up to 85 percent of the Latin Americans, 75 percent of the Poles and volunteers from the Balkans, around 70 percent of the US volunteers and 60 percent of the French volunteers were members of the Communist Party.[7]

More important in terms of Communist control of the International Brigades was the role played by military cadres sent from the Soviet Union by the Comintern. These included many Soviet citizens of foreign origin, who had ended up in Russia during the revolution, usually as prisoners of war, had joined the Communist Party and had become officers in the Red Army. One such case was that of General 'Emilio Kleber', the first commander of the International Brigades, who had been a former officer in the Austro-Hungarian army and had previously been sent by the Red Army as a military adviser to the Chinese Communists. Kleber had arrived in Spain on 15 September, that is three days before the Comintern's decision to organise the Brigades. Like other foreign Communists with military experience, he fought as an officer in the Communist led 5th Regiment. In late October, Kleber was proposed by the Spanish Communist Party to prime minister Largo Caballero as commander of the International Brigades.

Other Communist exiles sent by the Comintern to Spain, particularly those of German and Central European origin, had gone to the USSR for military training. Among these, for example, were several former leaders of the short lived Soviet Republic of Hungary of 1919. In all, about 500 to 600 International Brigaders had previously been in the Soviet Union.[8]

In addition to those who came directly from the USSR, Communist and other anti-fascist exiles, often resident in France, also volunteered to fight. The war in Spain gave them the perfect opportunity to fight back against fascism and to escape the indignities of exile life. As one German International Brigade commander, put it, 'The only way we can get back to Germany is through Madrid'.[9] The legal Communist parties also played an important role in recruiting volunteers. With the depression and the growing threat of fascism, followed by the turn to the Popular Front, most parties had grown spectacularly. PCF membership, for instance, had risen from 28,825 in 1933 to 254,000 by September 1936.[10] There appears to have been no shortage of volunteers at first and most parties turned men away. Like the anti-fascist exiles, many of those who went to Spain had fought in street battles against the fascists. Many US volunteers had experience of fighting the police 'anti-red' squads and bosses' thugs, or in the dangerous drives to organise black farm workers in the south. A few International Brigaders had played a leading role in military mutinies. For instance, the future commander in chief of the Brigades, André Marty, had been a leader of the famous Black Sea mutiny in the French navy in 1919.

The recruitment process in Britain was probably representative of what happened in most democracies. Recruitment was carried out discreetly, potential volunteers often being approached by local CP organisers, before being interviewed and warned of the dangers involved. Non-party volunteers were checked up on by trusted local party members. Both the US and British parties tried to avoid sending too many leading members. Upon leaving their countries volunteers were often harassed or even arrested by the police. This was the case both in the US and Britain where it was illegal to enlist in a foreign army and where the authorities were most determined to impose non-intervention. Given restrictions on the issuing of passports, British volunteers usually travelled on special weekend returns to France, for which passports were not necessary. Movement across France and into Spain was less complicated, due to the slightly more benevolent attitude of the French authorities and the influence of the PCF.

Of the estimated 53 nations from which volunteers came, the largest contingent was the French, about 9,000. There were also up to 5,000 Germans and Austrians, 3,000 Poles, 3,000 Italians, 2,800 Americans, 1,800 British, 1,600 Belgians, 1,660 Yugoslavs and 1,500

Czechoslovakians.[11] Even inside the different contingents there was often a wide range of nationalities. The US contingent was made up of volunteers from 35 different national groups. Of 1,448 Canadians who went to Spain there were at least 14 different ethnic groups represented and 498 were of Eastern European origin. Jews were particularly prominent in the International Brigades, making up between 30 to 40 percent of US volunteers and between 3,000 and 7,000 of the International Brigaders as a whole. There were 81 Afro-Americans in the Abraham Lincoln Battalion, nearly all of them Communists, and for the first time in US military history a black officer, Oliver Law, led white troops into battle.[12]

Because various well known intellectual figures participated in the Spanish Civil War as prominent supporters of the Republican cause, Stephen Spender's claim that it was a 'poet's war' has been given too much credibility. In fact, over 80 percent of the volunteers were from a manual working class background. Many were unemployed and most were young—the average age of US volunteers was 26.[13]

The revolutionary left and international volunteers

The sending of foreign volunteers was part of the massive solidarity campaigns that the left, especially the Communists, were organising throughout the world. For those who defended the revolutionary nature of the Spanish war—anarchists and revolutionary socialists—the most important act of solidarity was to fight for the revolution in their country of origin. However, there were volunteers from all revolutionary tendencies present in Spain, although their level of organisation could never match that of the Communists.

The powerful anarcho-syndicalist movement in Spain, the CNT, had an ambiguous attitude towards the question of foreign volunteers. In September 1936 the anarchist leader, Diego Abad de Santillán, publicly stated that the revolution needed arms, not foreign fighters, and gave orders to CNT militia guarding the frontier to stop any more international volunteers entering the country. Likewise, Durruti argued that solidarity work in France was more important than coming to Spain to fight. However, Abad de Santillán's orders seem to have had little effect and later the CNT press would praise the heroism of the International Brigades during the battle of Belchite. Despite the apparent lack of interest in getting foreign volunteers for its militias, some 2,000 foreign anarchists fought with the CNT, including about 500 Italians, 250 French and 230 Germans. In contrast to the Comintern, the anarchist international had no centralised recruitment campaign. Apart from refugees already living in Spain, the small French anarchist movement organised the sending of volunteers. Problems arose when in early 1937 the militias were militarised and integrated into the Popular Army which would not accept the existence of separate foreign units outside the International Brigades. As a result some of these anarchist volunteers left the country, others joined CNT led units in the new army and a few joined the International Brigades.[14]

Unlike the CNT, the POUM openly favoured the sending of foreign volunteers while at the same time defending the need to spread the revolution. As soon as the war started, the POUM appealed for international working class solidarity with the revolution, including the sending of aid and fighters. This call was taken up by the International Bureau for Revolutionary Socialist Unity which grouped together various left socialist and dissident communist organisations. Like the anarchists, the various small parties that made up the International Bureau were not in a position to send forces comparable to the International Brigades. Of the 9,000 to 10,000 militia organised by the POUM prior to its suppression in June 1937, up to 700 were foreign volunteers, from at least 25 different countries. Most of these fighters were political refugees, some already resident in Spain. About half were German and there were also significant groups of French and Italians. The British Independent Labour Party had a contingent of 30 on the Huesca front with the POUM forces after January 1937, including George Orwell. Among the foreign volunteers were some of the few militiamen with any previous military experience so they played an important role in the POUM's Lenin Division, both as officers and commissars. Two thirds of the division's crack Shock Battalion were foreigners, mostly Germans. Politically the international volunteers in the POUM militia were fairly heterogeneous, reflecting in many ways the party's own political confusion, and ranging from the centrist SAP and ILP through to a few Trotskyists and other revolutionaries. When the Lenin (29th) Division was dissolved in June 1937, many of the POUM's foreign volunteers had to flee the country to avoid arrest. Some were imprisoned but at least a few of the Germans were allowed into the International Brigades.[15]

Neither did the Trotskyists oppose sending volunteers to fight in Spain, although their aim was quite clearly to intervene politically in the revolution. In early August 1936 an agreement was reached between Jean Rous, the Trotskyist International Secretariat representative in Barcelona, and the POUM for foreign Trotskyists to join the party's militia. This led to the formation of the first exclusively international unit in the Republican zone, the International Lenin Column. The majority of its 50 fighters were Trotskyists or members of the Italian ultra-leftist Bordigist faction. But in late October the column dissolved itself after the Bordigists refused to return to the front because the

POUM had published the government's militarisation decree in its press. The Trotskyists did not follow the Bordigists in abandoning the country altogether. They mostly left the POUM militia to work in the rearguard or joined CNT units where they felt more useful political work could be carried out. The disbanding of the International Lenin Column coincided with the breakdown in relations between the POUM and various foreign Trotskyists working with it once the latter began to attack the POUM over its decision to participate in the Catalan government.

The military role of the International Brigades

The significance of the International Brigades' intervention in the civil war becomes clearer when the relatively small number of troops involved, their lack of military experience or sufficient training, the specific logistical problems involved in organising such a multinational force and the failings of their commanders are all taken into account. Their role as shock troops, thrown into the most vulnerable parts of the front line, meant their losses were much higher than most other units'. Their reliability in combat had as much to do with their political commitment as with military efficiency. Until the spring of 1937 at least, the International Brigades were a key element of the Republican forces, superior to the first Popular Army units.[16] As one historian put it, although 'it would be excessive to say that the presence [of the International Brigades] was decisive...they fought with so much faith, the psychological effect was considerable in a conflict in which symbolic values played a great role'.[17] Even after the Popular Army had become more effective, the International Brigades still played an active part in nearly all the remaining battles of the war.

Numerically, the International Brigades were fairly insignificant compared with the overall size of the Republican Army which consisted of 450,000 men by early 1938. Most histories speak of there having been 40,000 or more International Brigaders, but more recent research shows that this figure was much more likely to have been less than 30,000, of which only 18,000 were ever present at any one time, and this includes several hundred men and women who served in the Brigades' medical services and as drivers. Moreover, only a minority of the International Brigades were ready for combat and even less were at the front. André Marty reported to the Comintern in March 1937 that the International Brigade had 18,000 men, of which only half were ready for combat. By July 1937 22,000 men had passed through the Brigades' ranks, of which 7,000 had been casualties, 4,500 of those fatal, and there were less than 8,000 at the front. The arrival of new recruits over the summer of 1937 brought the total present since October 1936 to 24,464.[18] Levels of recruitment subsequently declined and never compensated for the constant stream of losses.

The majority of volunteers had no military experience. This lack of combat experience, which was hardly surprising given that it was nearly 20 years since the First World War, was only compensated for by the volunteers' participation in street fighting and, above all, by their political commitment. Of the British contingent around 30 percent claimed to be ex-servicemen, although one combatant, Jason Gurney, reckoned that 'more than 80 percent had never held a loaded weapon in their hands before'. The importance of their political commitment becomes apparent when one considers that, at least initially, the training given to the International Brigaders was very inadequate. At first the British volunteers were only shown how to advance over open country, not how to fortify a position and hold it or how to beat an organised retreat—with disastrous consequences on their first day in action. Likewise, the first US volunteers had 'no more than a few days training' before being sent to fight. In fact they had no firing practice at all until, on their way to the front, they were allowed to get out of their lorries and fire a few rounds into the surrounding hills before continuing on to their bloody initiation into the horrors of war.[19]

Like the rest of the Republican forces, the International Brigades initially suffered not only from a shortage of arms but the problems created by using different types of weapons and ammunition. Neither was it just arms that were lacking: when the US volunteers arrived at the Jarama front and were told to dig in, they discovered they had nothing to dig with. However, this would soon change with the steady arrival of new Soviet weapons, and the International Brigades 'despite deficiencies' were the 'best supplied in the Republican Army'. As Walter Gregory remembered, 'our rifles…were Soviet made and were identical to those used by the Red Army. They were brand new and were distributed straight from the packing cases in which they had come…a very good weapon.' The contrast with Orwell's description of the antiquated rifles available to the POUM militia on the Aragon front could not have been starker.[20]

Another problem faced by such a multinational force was that of communication, especially at the front when orders often had to be given rapidly over the phone. Volunteers were organised by language group in an attempt to overcome this problem, but inevitably this was only a partial solution. There was no attempt to teach the International Brigaders Spanish until early 1937 and few seem to have actually learnt it. The most commonly heard languages were French and German, given the predominance of volunteers who spoke these two languages. Among the general staff, reflecting the Soviet citizenship of many of its components, Russian was common.

The high casualty rate suffered by the International Brigades was mainly due to their role as shock troops. However, military inefficiency, common enough in most armies, and in this case often directly due to political reasons, was also part of the cause.[21] An estimated third of all international volunteers were killed and the majority of the rest wounded. According to one estimate, only 7 percent of the International Brigades left Spain unscathed. The death rate among different national groups appears to have differed due either to excessive confidence by the general staff or due to their national origin. Those who were refugees from authoritarian regimes appear to have been considered both more expendable and more reliable. So while the fatal casualty rate of US, British and French combatants was around 30 percent, still extremely high, 40 percent of Germans were killed, along with 48 percent of Yugoslavs and 42 percent of Hungarians. The exception was the Italians, of whom 'only' 18 percent died.[22]

The first intervention of the International Brigades, in the siege of Madrid on 8 November 1936, would become legendary. The first Brigade to arrive was the XI with 1,700 men, mainly Germans, French, Belgians and Poles, followed by the XII four days later with another 1,550. The CNT press in the capital reported their arrival in the early hours of the morning 'in silent and damp streets: Marching firmly, their footsteps echoing on the cobblestones…singing revolutionary songs in French, German, Italian… The people ran out to cheer them,' convinced these strangely uniformed men had been sent by Russia and 'if their powerful ally Russia…intervened on their side anything was possible…the cry rang out from many a balcony—Long live the Russians !' After two days of combat half the XI were dead. A few days later the XII was thrown into the battle, also sustaining heavy losses in the desperate room by room fighting on the university campus. The International Brigades did not save Madrid, as was subsequently made out by the Communists, for the militia and population had checked the main fascist advance the day before, but their bravery and example proved an important morale booster for the beleaguered Republican forces. A myth of invincibility was now built up around Kleber but, jealous of his popularity, the Communist Party had him removed from Madrid. In the summer of 1937, he was recalled to Moscow where he disappeared.[23]

In early 1937 the International Brigades were boosted by the arrival of more volunteers, including the first contingents sent from Britain and the US. A few weeks later the International Brigades played a small but important role in the Republic's major offensive at Jarama, plugging gaps in the front lines at key moments and once more showing outstanding courage. It was a baptism of fire for the US volunteers who were thrown straight into battle with very little preparation and suffered heavy losses;

of 450 men, 120 were killed and 170 wounded. The British Battalion was
also reduced to half its number in the first day's fighting at Jarama.[24] The
International Brigades' participation at Guadalajara in March would
prove even more decisive. This battle was particularly significant, apart
from being one of the Republic's few outright victories in the war,
because of Mussolini's insistence that the Italian Fascist forces should be
allowed to play a leading part in the offensive and thus show their military
superiority. According to the Italian Fascist Grand Council their victory
would mark the 'end of all Bolshevik plans in the West and the beginning
of a new era of power and social justice for the Spanish people'.[25] Instead
the battle turned into a humiliating defeat for the Italian High Command.
At the height of the fighting Italian anti-fascists clashed with Mussolini's
troops. The International Brigades brought up huge loudspeakers to
broadcast revolutionary songs and appeals in Italian to the Fascist soldiers
to lay down their arms. Leaflets, guaranteeing safe conduct to any Italian
soldiers who deserted and joined their working class brothers, were
dropped from planes and thrown across the lines wrapped around stones.
The eventual surrender of hundreds of demoralised Italian Fascist troops
was of great emotional and political significance for the Italian anti-
fascist exiles.

Guadalajara marked a watershed in the International Brigades' intervention in the Civil War. From now on the Brigades practically ceased to
be mentioned in the Republican press at all. Gone were the headlines
about the glorious International Brigades which had saved Madrid and
stemmed the fascist tide at Jarama. There were several reasons for this
change. In part it reflected the desperate attempts of the Popular Front
government to win support from the Western democracies by playing
down as far as possible foreign involvement on the Republican side,
especially after the decision by the Non-Intervention Committee in
February 1937 to prohibit all recruitment for Spain. It was also the
logical consequence of the Popular Front political argument that increasingly emphasised the 'national' element of the Republic's struggle
against the foreign fascist aggressor aided by a small clique of traitorous
Spanish generals. By 1938, this patriotic stance had led to the war being
described as one for 'national independence' with continued parallels
made with the War of Independence against the French at the beginning
of the 19th century. In such a war the participation of an internationalist
and Communist led force such as the International Brigades had to be
played down if not totally hidden. The growing efficiency of the
Republic's new Popular Army also meant that the International
Brigades' role was less noticeable. Few International Brigaders seem to
have been aware of their changing role. The significance of their lack of
awareness of how they were perceived officially by the Republican

authorities is one of the more glaring examples of their isolation from the
political reality of the country; something which would prove very useful
in sustaining the Popular Front view of what the war was really about.[26]

Another serious problem for the International Brigades was the drop-
ping off of recruitment. Between April and September 1937, 6,464 new
recruits arrived in Albacete, compared with 18,000 during the first six
months of the International Brigades' existence.[27] The Non-Intervention
Committee's determination to stop all foreign recruitment was central to
this drop in the number of fresh volunteers. News of the terrible casualties
in the International Brigades' first engagements also deterred would-be
volunteers. The outbreak of internecine fighting in the Republican zone in
May 1937 and the growing evidence of Stalinist repression contributed to
undermining the appeal of the International Brigades to non-Communist
volunteers. From now on the International Brigades were increasingly
boosted by Spanish conscripts, who eventually made up the majority of the
Brigades' troops. A new Comintern campaign for volunteers in September
did not stem this downward trend. By July 1938 the integration of Spanish
conscripts into the International Brigades was such that, of their 40,149
troops, only 14,175 were foreigners. But, despite growing demoralisation,
falling recruitment and political relegation, they participated, with terrible
losses, in all the remaining major engagements of the war. The relative
importance of the International Brigades to the Republican war effort was
well illustrated at Teruel when they were brought into the front line once
the fascists began to break through in January 1938, despite the
Republican minister of war's declared intention of using only local troops
in this latest offensive, in an attempt to prove the patriotic nature of his
government's struggle.

Revolution and counter-revolution

Although the International Brigades as such did not intervene directly in
the suppression of the revolution, British volunteers arriving in
Barcelona in May 1937 were asked whether they would be prepared to
participate in the street fighting on the side of government forces if the
situation got worse.[28] Foreign members of various security services,
usually NKVD agents, were active both inside the International Brigades
and in the rearguard against the revolutionary left. The German
Communist Party, the KPD, had its own secret intelligence agency inside
the International Brigades, which collected information on Nazi spies
and revolutionaries alike and during the May fighting was involved in
arresting German anarchists. Other Comintern cadres, some members of
the International Brigades, were involved with the Communist run 'State
Information Group' which was used against foreign dissidents, as well as

local anarchists and 'Trotskyists'.[29]

From the International Brigaders' own memoirs it is clear how little they understood what was really happening in Spain. This was due both to the overwhelming influence of the Communists and to the isolation of most of them from the rest of the population, be it as a result of language problems, the length of time spent at the front or a deliberate policy.[30] The situation which Walter Gregory found himself in was typical of many others: 'Looking back...it is astonishing how little I knew of Spain. I did not appreciate its form of government at all and was content simply to label it as 'democratic'... [I had] no real knowledge of [the] groups which were engaged in the struggle for power'.[31] Few International Brigaders would have had any alternative source of information about divisions inside the world Communist movement or anything approaching the truth about the purges then taking place in the USSR. In the heat of battle, most foreign volunteers readily accepted that any criticism of the Popular Front was playing into the hands of fascism.

The International Brigade press, like its Communist counterpart, slavishly followed the line from Moscow that Trotsky and his followers were fascist agents and that all dissident voices, real or imagined, inside the Communist movement were 'Trotskyists'. In the Spanish context the increasingly hysterical attacks on the 'Trotsky-fascist POUM' by early 1937 were preparing the ground for a more decisive offensive against this party and the revolution in general. The leadership of the International Brigades clearly understood the political aspect of their intervention on certain fronts. When Kleber was sent to participate in the offensive on Zaragoza, he reported to the Comintern that these operations gave the Communist Party 'the chance to finish with anarcho-Trotskyist-fascist domination in Aragon'.[32] The International Brigade newspaper claimed in February 1937 that after the Moscow trial 'the whole world can see' that the Trotskyists were 'agents of German-Japanese fascism...an incredible system of provocations, sabotage and murder', and in Spain, they had been revealed as 'the artificial mist that hid Franco's Fifth Column'. The 'unmasking of the Trotskyists' united all International Brigaders.[33]

When the fighting broke out between the anarchists and the POUM on one side, and the Popular Front government and Communist Party on the other in Barcelona in May 1937 it was at a time of general demoralisation at the front and the International Brigade leadership had little difficulty in convincing most volunteers that it was the work of Franco's agents. What happened inside the Lincoln Battalion was probably representative of other units. Robert Minor, the US representative of the Comintern, addressed the battalion for two hours on how the Trotskyists were really in the pay of the fascists. Edwin Rolfe wrote home, 'If you were here you would understand why it isn't enough to be passively bitter or politically opposed to these bastards… Their stinking pro-fascist actions here should convince anyone who really is for the workers that they're fit only to be spat on, crushed'.[34] Of those International Brigaders involved more directly in the repression, however, not all remained loyal to Stalin. Hubert von Ranke, part of the KPD's security operation in Spain, fled to Paris in November 1937, broke with the party and announced that the people he had helped repress in Barcelona 'were not agents of Franco but honest revolutionaries'.[35]

The virulent anti-Trotskyism of the International Brigade press was the other side of the coin to its passionate defence of the Popular Front. 'Collectively, [the International Brigades] constituted one of the most powerful symbols of the urgent anti-fascist message that the USSR tried to transmit to the Western democracies', and with this in mind, 'the Communists set about the task of creating myths about the Brigades.' The very name, 'Volunteers for Liberty', by which the Brigades were known, encapsulated the politics of an anti-fascist alliance that aimed to unite all democrats. The US Communists chose the names of Lincoln and Washington for their battalions to reflect the democratic, and even patriotic, nature of their struggle, rather than that of the imprisoned labour leader Tom Mooney whose case was considered 'too inflammatory'.[36]

Since the war some former International Brigaders have played an important role in trying to sustain the Popular Front and Stalinist view of events. One Scottish volunteer would still insist 40 years later that 'the terrible crime of the POUM' was that it 'tried to foster the idea that this was a revolutionary war…it never had any signs of a revolutionary war…they were people concerned to expel the Italians and Germans', the war was 'a revolt against an invasion by foreigners…sponsored by a handful of generals led by Franco'.[37] Likewise, the reaction of former International Brigaders to Ken Loach's film *Land and Freedom* as a 'distortion of history', that 'slanders' the International Brigades by accusing them of being controlled by the Stalinists, is only part of a long and sad history of denunciations of any view that challenges the Popular Front myths about the civil war. George Orwell's *Homage to Catalonia*, on which Loach's film is loosely based, has been singled out by the last commander of the British Battalion, Bill Alexander, as being 'bitterly anti-Republican…muck and fantasy'.[38]

Despite sustaining this virulent defence of the Popular Front line since the late 1930s, many Communists at the time had a more contradictory view of what they were doing. Most rank and file Communists saw themselves as revolutionaries and the Popular Front as a necessary tactical interlude before the implantation of proletarian dictatorship. This belief was encouraged by the relatively recent experience of the October Revolution in Russia and the widespread conviction, not only among

Communists, that the USSR was a socialist state. It also helps explain the hold of Stalinism over important sectors of the most militant workers in the 1930s. The subsequent development of the Communist parties would see these long term revolutionary aims become even more abstract, but in the 1930s such ideas were still fairly central to the commitment of many of their members.

This contradictory view of their role was clear among the International Brigaders, even taking into account their disciplined defence of the Comintern position and their limited understanding of the political situation in Spain. Many US volunteers, for instance, 'defined their mission in revolutionary terms'. Political commissar Sandor Voros would claim years later that he went to Spain 'to fight under the leadership of the Comintern, the giants of the revolution', that he was part of 'the expression of international solidarity forged by the Comintern into an armoured fist of the revolutionary working class'.[39] Even more significantly, the International Brigades' officers and commissars often appealed to their men's revolutionary consciousness in order to lift morale. Thus Robert Minor addressed the Lincoln Battalion as 'the cadres of the international revolution' and Kleber urged the surviving International Brigaders into yet another attack on the Madrid front with a resounding 'For the revolution and liberty—forward !'[40]

Repression inside the International Brigades

Many hostile sources talk of the 'reign of terror' which supposedly existed within the International Brigades, especially at their base in Albacete. Sandros Voros, after he had turned against the Communists, claimed that officers and soldiers of the International Brigades were 'implacably executed following Kremlin orders'. André Marty is singled out in particular as responsible for this repression, and was labelled the 'Butcher of Albacete' by right wing French parliamentary deputies, a name subsequently taken up by embittered former Communists and the writer Ernest Hemingway. What is clear is that Marty was both incompetent as a military leader and obsessed to the point of paranoia about the threat of infiltration by spies and 'Trotskyists'. According to the International Brigade commander in chief, all foreign espionage organisations were at work in the Brigades, 'above all the Deuxième Bureau of the French General Staff'. However, it is misleading to put what repression that did take place solely down to the 'demented Marty'.[41]

The extent of the repression inside the International Brigades, and Marty's role in it, is open to debate, but what is clear is the complex security structure which operated inside their ranks. Most of those who had a leading role inside these structures were foreign Communists sent by the

Comintern, usually connected in one way or another to the NKVD and often involved in counter-espionage activities outside the International Brigades. Apart from the KPD's own secret service, the first organism used to control foreign volunteers was the Catalan Communist Party (the PSUC) Foreigners' Bureau in Barcelona to which new volunteers in the autumn of 1936 surrendered their passports and which was run by foreign Communists and the NKVD. It was later used to organise expulsions, torture and even the murder of both foreign and Spanish dissidents. It was not long before the International Brigades had their own security service. In January 1937 Marty reported to the Comintern that the International Brigades were setting up a 'Control and Security Service' with the collaboration of 'two Mexican [Russian] comrades'. One was probably Alexander Orlov, head of the NKVD's operation in Spain.[42]

A 'Cadre Commission' was established at Albacete in February which would be the main body responsible for surveillance inside the International Brigades until the creation of the Republican counter-espionage service, the SIM, six months later. Similar cadre commissions had existed in the Russian Communist Party since 1922 and inside the Comintern after 1932 and played a very important role in monitoring party members' trustworthiness. The commission's principal task was to select and promote the best volunteers, as well as unmask any *provocateurs*. Nearly all the heads of this commission were experienced Comintern cadres, had worked in its cadre section in Moscow and usually had studied at Soviet military schools. After a time the most important linguistic groups had their own commissions. By 1938, the Cadre Commission had 83 collaborators, most of whom were Communists and had previously been at the front. A report on 362 British volunteers, half of them Communists, gives an insight into the commission's work. The report describes 31 of them as 'cadres', 142 as being reliable, and 133, of which 40 were party members, as 'weak or bad'. When the SIM was established inside the International Brigades, it was made up of mainly foreign Communists and its activities overlapped with the Cadre Commission.[43]

Most punitive action inside the International Brigades, as in most armies, was taken in response to indiscipline and desertion: two 're-education centres' and three jails were established at Albacete to deal with such cases.[44] By the spring of 1937 the harsh realities of the war in Spain had become very clear to the volunteers and desertions began to increase. Long inactive stretches in the front lines without leave added to the general demoralisation in the ranks, leading to desertion, insubordination and growing rivalries between national groups. Marty reported to the Comintern after the battles of Jarama and Guadalajara that the Brigades were on the verge of falling apart, such was the level of demoralisation and the loss of men through both casualties and desertion. The change in the situation inside the International Brigades after Guadalajara is clearly reflected in reports to Moscow, where the same men previously praised for their courage at the front are now described as 'cowards, amoral and alcoholics'. One of the more dramatic examples of insubordination took place during the disastrous attack on Brunete in July 1937, when the Polish and Slav units refused to return to the front and discipline was only re-established with the arrival of Assault Guards (Republican police) and tanks. There were also outbreaks of indiscipline and desertion among the British and Americans after Brunete, as there had been at Jarama. By August 1937, according to Marty, 'most battalions were down to less than 200 men, volunteers were tired and there were 'constant desertions…especially among the French and English'. In October, Marty accused the commander of the French-Belgian Brigade of 'organising mass desertions' after half the men in two battalions had abandoned their units in three weeks.[45]

Given the terrible conditions in which the International Brigades fought, the number of desertions was not that great, a further reflection of the deep political commitment of the majority of the volunteers. An estimated 298 British volunteers deserted (16 percent), compared with about 100 Americans (3.5 percent), who would not have found it so easy to return home. The fate of captured deserters appears to have been mixed. They were usually held in penal battalions, often set to work digging trenches, and eventually released, but, according to Jason Gurney, 'a large number disappeared without trace'. Apart from desertion and insubordination, in the town of Albacete there were numerous cases brought before the local courts of public disorder and even homicide involving International Brigaders.[46]

Reprisals for political dissent were less common than punishment for indiscipline, but have attracted more attention, if only because of Marty's obsession with unmasking spies and Trotskyists. In October 1937 Marty complained to Moscow of 'foreign centres', especially Lyon, Paris and Nice, from where the 'infiltration of provocateurs' was organised with the recruitment of 'alcoholics, Trotskyists and anarchists'. In this atmosphere, with the daily attacks on Trotskyists, real and otherwise, in the International Brigade and Communist press as fascist agents, not surprisingly any dissident was quickly denounced as a 'Trotskyist' and often arrested. The Comintern Executive Committee in September 1937 exhorted all officers and men of the International Brigades to fight against 'Trotskyist-fascist' infiltration. But there were very few real Trotskyists in the International Brigades. One was the Brazilian officer, August Besought, who was murdered by the NKVD. The Danish Trotskyist, Aage Kielso, fought with the International Brigades on the Madrid and Córdoba fronts. Those few anarchists who enlisted in the

International Brigades were 'strictly controlled by the SIM'.[47]

The exact number of International Brigaders executed is hard to ascertain. One sympathetic history says there were around 50 executions, giving details of 25 of these. The true figure was probably higher.[48] At Albacete there was a 'legal commission', really a council of war, which handed out death penalties. The condemned men were usually accused of cowardice or of being spies, *provocateurs* or Trotskyists. What does seem clear is that the punishment meted out to volunteers differed depending on nationality. Marty was particularly critical of the Belgians and French, who as a consequence were often among those arrested. Volunteers who were political exiles from authoritarian regimes also seem to have suffered disproportionately, especially those from Moscow, as there would be no redress from prying governments. Various International Brigade cadre would be executed upon returning to Moscow, as happened with some of the Soviet military advisers. One of the more dramatic examples of repression was that of nine Germans shot during the battle of Teruel for having tried to incite their comrades to disobey orders. In contrast, the Americans and British came off lightly. Among the US volunteers there are only three known cases of executions and the British only one, and even this case is disputed.[49]

The effects of this repressive atmosphere, combined with military inefficiency, undermined morale even further, especially among the non-Communist volunteers. According to Gurney, the 'pattern of unkept promises of support, chaotic orders and communications, followed by inquests, the finding of scapegoats and their execution as enemy agents was to underlie the whole course of events.' Or as one US volunteer recalled, 'It was one of the most poignant and tragic experiences of the men who volunteered for the International Brigades, to find out that they could be as greatly defeated by the remote control of the Kremlin as by the Non-Intervention Pact'.[50]

The end of the Brigades

By June 1938 the Soviet government was considering abandoning the Republic, both because of its failure to establish an anti-Hitler alliance with the Western governments and because a fascist victory looked increasingly inevitable. About this time the Soviet foreign minister Litvinov told the British ambassador that a Franco regime was acceptable provided it did not become a German or Italian satellite.[51] The Soviet representative on the Non-Intervention Committee agreed to the drawing up of a plan for the withdrawal of all foreign combatants in Spain and the granting of belligerent rights to both sides—allowing them to buy arms legally. The proposed plan for withdrawal included the far greater forces fighting on Franco's side. However, given the complete cynicism with which the fascist powers had treated the Non-Intervention Committee since its formation, few could have seriously thought that they would carry out their side of any agreement.

On 21 September, in a last desperate attempt to win the support of the Western governments, the president of the Republic, Juan Negrín, announced at the League of Nations, while the decisive battle of the Ebro was still being fought, his government's unilateral decision to withdraw all foreign combatants from the Republican zone. Of the 12,673 foreign volunteers left in the Republican Army, 7,000 fought in the Ebro offensive—75 percent of them becoming casualties.[52] The Republican side now lost a small, but important, minority of experienced fighters. The positions handed over by the International Brigades were soon lost and by 18 November, the Republicans held no point on the southern bank of the Ebro.

The actual evacuation of the International Brigaders was not easy and by January 1939 only 4,640 had left. About 6,000 volunteers remained demobilised in Catalonia. As the region fell, the Communist Party called on the remaining International Brigaders to re-enlist. Eighty percent did so, fighting in the desperate rearguard actions as the Republican forces and hundreds of thousands of refugees fled towards the border. On 9 February the International Brigaders were among the last Republican troops to cross the border.[53] On 24 February, France recognised the Franco government and three days later Britain did the same.

The story of the International Brigades does not finish with the end of the Spanish Civil War. Their odyssey would continue in the prison camps of Franco's Spain and Nazi Germany, in the forefront of the anti-fascist resistance and in the allied armed forces. Others would perish in the Stalinist purges in the USSR or the post-war regimes of Eastern Europe—the very fact they had been in Spain made them a threat. A few would escape the purges to become political and military leaders in the new Soviet bloc. In the West they would also be persecuted, particularly in the US where they were accused of being 'premature anti-fascists'; others would end up in the leadership of the trade unions or as political leaders of the left. Some would turn against their past and become right wing anti-communists or, in a few cases, join revolutionary groups.

The legacy of the International Brigades

The legacy of the International Brigades is contradictory. Their intervention in the civil war not only directly aided the Republic in its fight against fascism but also boosted the credibility of the Communist parties. As one British historian wrote, 'The unquestioned bravery and sincerity of these men did much to enhance the reputation of the Communist Party among those members of the battalion who held other views and at the same time had a great propaganda value in Britain itself... As the civil war progressed the idealism and heroism of the Battalion had an ever greater impact on the labour movement, with the resulting rapid increase in the membership and influence of the Communist Party'.[54] In particular, this prestige was used to justify the Stalinist popular front strategy. The class collaboration and reformism enshrined in this strategy have been a hallmark of Communist Party politics ever since.

For revolutionary socialists, the question arises of whether volunteers should have gone to Spain. Should not the task of socialists have been first and foremost to have fought for the revolution in their own countries as the most effective way of supporting Spanish workers? Although this is undoubtedly the case, there were also important reasons for socialists to have considered volunteering. At a practical level, there were German and Italian exiles who were unable to fight in their own countries. More importantly, the workers' organisations in Spain, with the exception of some sectors of the anarchists, wanted volunteers to come and fight. The real problem was the political context in which the International Brigades intervened. The participation of international volunteers on the side of the Republic was only really openly used to bolster morale during the first months when they were present, after which they virtually disappeared from public view so as not to alarm the democracies too much and above all to reinforce the propaganda that this was a war for 'national independence' against foreign (Italian and German) invaders. If the volunteers had returned to their countries to explain the revolutionary nature of the Spanish war, their role in their respective labour movements would have been very different.

Despite the obvious weaknesses of the International Brigades' politics, for the left today they remain one of the most impressive and heroic examples of working class internationalism and anti-fascism. As US volunteer and life-long Communist, Alvah Bessie, wrote, 'In the history of the world there had never existed a group of men like this...an international army formed...by volunteers from all walks of life. The actual existence of this army...was a guarantee of the brotherhood of the international working class, the definitive proof that [the workers] have a common interest and obligation'.[55] This internationalism could not have contrasted more strongly with the treacherous policies of the bourgeois democracies and their political supporters, both left and right, who preferred the Republic to fall rather than themselves make a stand against fascism. Despite being relatively few in number, the International Brigades played a relatively important role as shock troops. Their political commitment and revolutionary consciousness, despite the treacherous role of their Stalinist leaders, were central to their effectiveness and for this they paid a heavy price. The fact that many International Brigaders were later persecuted by democratic governments, and by fascist and Stalinist regimes alike, is the clearest testimony to the example they provide to anyone who seeks to rid the world of injustice.

Notes

I am indebted to Mike Eaude for his valuable comments on the text.

1   J Esteban, 'Las Brigadas Internacionales y la Guerra Civil en la Literatura', in M Requena Gallego (ed), *La Guerra Civil Española y las Brigadas Internacionales* (Cuenca, 1998), p133.
2   W Gregory, *The Shallow Grave* (Nottingham, 1996), p20.
3   D Nelles, 'The Foreign Legion of the Revolution: German Anarchosyndicalists and Volunteers in Anarchist Militias during the Spanish Civil War', presented at the *Colloque International sur les Brigades Internationales* (CIBI) (Lausanne, 18-20 December 1997), p12.
4   M Alpert, *A New International History of the Spanish Civil War* (London, 1994), p51.
5   See G Howson, *Arms For Spain* (London, 1998).
6   P Broué, 'L'Internationale Communiste et les Brigades Internationales' (CIBI), p3.
7   P Pagès, 'Marty, Vidal, Kleber et le Komintern. Ce que nous apprennent les Archives de Moscou' (CIBI), pp5,16; G G Baumann, *Los Voluntarios Latinoamericanos en la Guerra Civil Española* (San José, 1997), pp212-244; P N Carroll, *The Odyssey of the Abraham Lincoln Brigade* (Stanford, 1994), p19; R Skoutelsky, 'L'engagement des volontaires français en Espagne républicaine' (CIBI), p12.
8   P Broué, op cit, pp3-5; Pagès, op cit, p17; W G Krivitsky, *I was Stalin's Agent* (Cambridge, 1992), p105.
9   H Beimler cited by G Regler, *The Owl of Minerva* (London, 1959).
10   R Skoutelsky, op cit, p14.
11   According to André Marty, S Álvarez, *Historia Política y Militar de las Brigadas Internacionales* (Madrid 1996) p309; P N Carroll, op cit, p65; J Gotovitch, 'Les volontaires de Belgique dans les Brigades. Quelques éléments pour une comparaison' (CIBI), p4; A Lesnik, 'Yugoslav Volunteers in the Spanish Civil War' (CIBI), p1.
12   P N Carroll, op cit, p18; J N McCrorie, 'Canadian Volunteers in the International Brigades : Spain 1936-1939' (CIBI), p10; *The Volunteer* (May, 1990).
13   T Buchanan, *Britain and the Spanish Civil War* (Cambridge, 1997), p126; H Thomas, *The Spanish Civil War* (Harmondsworth, 1971), p382; R Skoutelsky, op cit, p7; P N Carroll, op cit, p16.
14   A de Santillan, *Por qué Perdimos la Guerra* (Buenos Aires, 1940), p175; D Nelles, op cit, pp7,13; D Berry, 'Contribution to a Collective Biography of the French Anarchist Movement: French Anarchist Volunteers in Spain 1936-39' (CIBI), pp9-10.
15   A Durgan, 'International Volunteers in the POUM militias' (CIBI).
16   G Cardona, 'Las Brigadas Internacionales y el Ejército Popular' in M Requena Gallego, op cit, p76.
17   P Vilar, *La Guerra Civil Española* (Barcelona, 1986), p76.

18   P Pagès, op cit, pp5, 14-15; C Vidal, *Las Brigadas Internacionales* (Madrid, 1998), pp532-534, gives figures from a wide range of sources, from 120,000 according to the fascists to 25,000 in some Stalinist accounts.

19   T Buchanan, op cit, p127; J Gurney, *Crusade in Spain* (Newton Abbot, 1976), pp76,87; P N Carroll, op cit, pp95,100; A London, *Se levantaron antes del Alba...* (Barcelona, 1978), p86.

20   P N Carroll, op cit, p99; G Cardona, op cit, p76; W Gregory, op cit, p29; G Orwell, *Homage to Catalonia* (Harmondsworth, 1975), p35.

21   The opinion of former International Brigade commander Vital Gayman (Vidal), cited in P Broué, op cit, pp8-9; also see C Vidal, op cit, pp125-126.

22   S Alvarez, op cit, pp398-9; P N Carroll, op cit, p204; A Lesnik, op cit, p1; I Harsányi, 'Participación de Húngaros en las Brigadas Internacionales en restrospectiva histórica' (CIBI), p3; B H Bayerlein, 'Le Komintern, les Brigades Internationales en Espagne et le Parti Communiste Allemand' (CIBI), p14; H Thomas, op cit, p796.

23   H Thomas, op cit, p504; G Cardona, op cit, p76.

24   H Thomas, op cit, p491; J Gurney, op cit, pp127, 152; T Buchanan, op cit, p134.

25   P Broué and E Témime, *The Revolution and the Civil War in Spain* (London, 1972), pp258-259.

26   G Cardona, op cit, p76; M Requena Gallego, 'Albacete, Base de las Brigadas Internacionales 1936-1938', in M Requena Gallego (ed), op cit, p149.

27   P Pagès, op cit, pp14-15.

28   Hugh Sloan in I MacDougall (ed), *Voices from the Spanish Civil War* (Edinburgh, 1986), p199; William Herrick in his memoirs claims that several US volunteers were sent to the outskirts of Barcelona to take part in the repression—W Herrick, *Jumping the Line* (Wisconsin, 1998), p217.

29   D Nelles, op cit, p10; P Huber, 'Surveillance et répression politique dans les Brigades Internationales' (CIBI), p2.

30   G Cardona, op cit, p75; 'I lived in Spain some nine months, and had not made friends with one Spaniard. I hardly knew what a Spanish man or woman thought, except by what I read in the papers'—W Herrick, op cit, p220.

31   W Gregory, op cit, p19.

32   P Pagès, op cit, p21.

33   *Soldado de la República*, 16 February 1937.

34   P N Carroll, op cit, p83.

35   P Huber, op cit, p2.

36   G Esenwein, 'El Frente Popular: la política republicana durante la Guerra Civil', S Payne and J Tusell (eds), *La Guerra Civil. Una vision nueva del conflicto que dividio España* (Madrid, 1996), p369; C Almuiña Fernández and R M Martín de las Guardia, 'Prensa y propaganda durante la Guerra Civil: el mito de las Brigadas Internacionales', M Requena Gallego (ed), op cit, p325.

37   Tom Murray in I MacDougall (ed), op cit, p325.

38   B Alexander, 'Loach's film distorts history', *Morning Star,* 7 October 1995; B Alexander, 'Comments on A Moment of War', 6 November 1991 (unpublished); also see B Alexander, 'George Orwell and Spain' in C Norris (ed), *Inside the Myth—Orwell: Views from the Left* (London, 1984), pp85-102. Alexander has recently tried to discredit the writer Laurie Lee's critical account of his limited involvement in the war; while some of Lee's recollections are questionable, the claim by Alexander that Lee was never even in the Brigades is based on very slim evidence indeed—L Lee, *A Moment of War* (London, 1992); Alexander's opinion can be found in S Courtland, 'A not very Franco account', *The Spectator,* 3 January 1998; for a defence of Lee, M Eaude, 'Fighter or faker?', *The Guardian,* 13 May 1998.

39   P N Carroll, op cit, p130; S Voros, *American Commissar* (Philadelphia, 1961), p283.

40   P N Carroll, op cit, p161; A Malraux cited in H Thomas, op cit, p332.
41   S Voros, op cit, p410; P Broué and Témime, op cit, p388f; J Delperrie de Bayac, *Las Brigadas Internacionales* (Madrid, 1980), pp152-157; P Huber, op cit, pp5,7-9; J Gurney, op cit, p184.
42   P Huber, op cit, pp7-8.
43   Ibid, pp5-6; B Bayerlein, op cit, p6; P Broué, op cit, p7; Among the more notorious NKVD agents present in the International Brigades was the Polish Mickíewicz Battalion Commissar, Léon Narwicz, who would later infiltrate the POUM claiming to be a dissident Russian Red Army officer. Narwicz was later executed by a POUM action squad as a reprisal for the murder of Andréu Nin.
44   M Requena Gallego, op cit, p160; J Delperrie de Bayac, op cit, p157.
45   B Bayerlein, op cit, pp6, 10; P Pagès, op cit, pp5, 7, 13; H Thomas, op cit, pp591-592; Vidal, op cit, pp126, 274.
46   B Alexander, *British Volunteer for Liberty. Spain 1936-39* (London, 1982), p81; P N Carroll, op cit, p148; Gurney, op cit, p141; M Requena Gallego, op cit, p160.
47   B Bayerlein, op cit, p11; P Broué, op cit, p7; A Guillamón, *Documentación Histórica del trosquismo español (1936-1948)* (Madrid, 1996), p17; D Nelles, op cit, p18.
48   J Delperrie de Bayac, op cit, p145. Hostile accounts, without giving their source, claim that Marty admitted to the PCF Central Committee in November 1937 having ordered the execution of 500 men—J Gurney p144; C Vidal pp127, 351, 367; this information seems to originally have come from fascist sources, for example, 'Comité de Información y Actuación Social', *Las Brigadas Internacionales según testimonio de sus artifices* (Barcelona, nd, 1939/40), p23.
49   P Pagès, op cit, pp7-8,18; P Huber, op cit, p5; J Delperrie de Bayac, op cit, p151; B Alexander, *British Volunteers*, op cit, pp81-82; P N Carroll, op cit, pp187-8; M Requena Gallego, op cit, p159. According to Voros, Germans, Hungarians, Poles and Slavs were the main victims of execution—S Voros, op cit, pp410-411.
50   J Gurney, op cit, p82; P N Carroll, op cit, p239.
51   M Alpert, op cit, p148.
52   H Thomas, op cit, p704; G Cardona, op cit, p81; C Vidal, op cit, pp304-5.
53   A London, op cit, p302; J Delperrie de Bayac, op cit, pp317-318.
54   K W Watkins, *Britain Divided. The Effect of the Spanish Civil War on British Political Opinion* (London, 1963), p176.
55   A Bessie, *Men in Battle* (New York, 1939), p343.

Art, alienation and capitalism: a reply to Chris Nineham

JOHN MOLYNEUX

Chris Nineham's critical response ('Art and Alienation: A Reply to John Molyneux', *International Socialism* 82) to my article on 'The Legitimacy of Modern Art' is welcome because one of the main purposes of that article was to stimulate debate in an area in which there is not and cannot be an agreed 'line' and because it allows me to clarify a number of mis-understandings or misreadings that have evidently arisen regarding my position on art and alienation.

Especially welcome is the casual 'of course' in Chris's opening dec-laration that it 'is, of course, right to defend the validity of modern art against anyone who rejects it outright as a fraud or condemns it all for being unrealistic'.[1] If that is how things now stand, I am delighted. I have to say it was not quite how they looked to me when I embarked on this project some 18 months ago. Nor was it the hostility of the likes of Roger Scruton that was my main concern. Rather at that time it seemed a serious argument was required to persuade not all, but a substantial pro-portion of *International Socialism* readers that contemporary visual art was worth serious consideration. I think also that I should concede the accuracy of Chris's criticism that I overstated 'the level of mainstream hostility to contemporary art'.[2] This is a question of degree, for there is certainly quite a lot of such hostility still around, but he is right that it has lessened markedly in recent years and that in quite wide circles modern art is currently very fashionable.

But however much I welcome the debate I cannot agree with the main thrust of Chris's critique. Stripped of all extraneous elements, subsidiary comments and historical illustration this critique is as follows: (i) my definition of art as a product of unalienated labour is false because alienation is rooted in capitalist exploitation and capitalist relations of production and no aspect of society or part of the production process can escape the alienation imposed by the capitalist market; (ii) my definition of art is not only false but dangerous because it encourages or runs the risk of encouraging an attitude to art which is uncritical, elitist and ahistorical.

Before offering a response to these points I must note a peculiarity in the way Chris approaches this whole issue: namely he criticises my definition of art but offers no alternative definition of his own. He worries repeatedly about the 'risks' involved in my position, but seems to think he can avoid those risks himself by taking no position at all. Perhaps he thinks it is satisfactory to rely on a 'common sense' definition of art but surely he must realise that on this question, as on so many others, the common sense definition is going to be a bourgeois one. (I, at least, attempted a specifically Marxist definition using specifically Marxist categories.) Perhaps he thinks no definition is necessary or possible. This is an arguable, though in my opinion mistaken, position but Chris does not argue it. He simply fails to acknowledge the problem. But there is a problem—a real problem.

The reactionary opponents of modern art argue again and again that modernist works are *not art*. This was the case made against Brancusi,[3] against Pollock, against Carl Andre's 'bricks in the Tate' and, of course, against Hirst. Nor is it just a question of the opponents. Many of the leading practitioners of modernism have clearly been addressing this question themselves—think of Duchamp with his readymades, of surrealism, minimalism, pop art, conceptual art and so on. Each of these movements has overthrown accepted 'conventions' or 'definitions' of art. Each has defiantly addressed critic and public alike with the challenge, 'So you think you know what art is—look at this!' Therefore the question cannot be ignored. If we are going to discuss art and art works we need criteria for distinguishing art from non-art. Naturally I understand that the question is a difficult one or rather that answering it is difficult and I have no problem in accepting that my definition may be flawed or incomplete. I can even accept that it is completely wrong—on one condition: that I am shown a better one. This is a task Chris has not even attempted.

On the question of whether or not art is a product of unalienated labour let me begin by returning again to Marx's analysis of alienated labour in the *1844 Manuscripts*:

What constitutes the alienation of labour? First, that the work is external to the worker, that it is not part of his nature; and that, consequently, he does not fulfil himself in his work but denies himself, has a feeling of misery rather than well-being, does not develop freely his mental and physical energies but is physically exhausted and mentally debased. The worker, therefore, feels himself at home only during his leisure time, whereas at work he feels homeless. His work is not voluntary but imposed, forced labour. It is not the satisfaction of a need, but only a means for satisfying other needs. Its alien character is clearly shown by the fact that as soon as there is no physical or other compulsion it is avoided like the plague. External labour, labour in which man alienates himself, is a labour of self sacrifice, of mortification. Finally, the external character of work for the worker is shown by the fact that it is not his own work but work for someone else, that in work he does not belong to himself but to another person.[4]

Do any or all of these primary characteristics of alienated labour apply to artistic work. Plainly they do not. Michelangelo was sculpting, carving marble, to within four days of his death at the age of 89. Was this for the money? Not at all. Was it work in which he denied himself or was mentally debased? The opposite is the case. Was it 'imposed forced labour' or labour 'avoided like the plague' in the absence 'of physical or other compulsion'? Absolutely not. But is Michelangelo exceptional in this respect? No: Titian, Monet, Renoir, Picasso, Matisse, Moore and innumerable other artists worked on into extreme old age and infirmity long after any material pressure on them to do so had disappeared. Renoir is a case in point. In his last years he was crippled by arthritis, yet continued to paint with the brushes wedged between his twisted fingers. Was this alienated labour or was this because painting was essential to his being? The answer is obvious.

These examples do not, by themselves, prove my case—even if these artists' work was unalienated labour this may not be true for all or most art—but they do refute a major part of Chris Nineham's case because his argument is that, under capitalism, unalienated labour is impossible. ('...under capitalism no part of the production process can escape the alienation imposed by the capitalist market'.[5])

On this point Chris is simply wrong. Of course under capitalism the *majority* of labour and the characteristic *form* of labour is alienated wage labour but this does not make all labour under capitalism alienated. As a university lecturer I have a relatively 'soft' job with a relatively high degree of autonomy. Nevertheless I am acutely aware of the distinction between the alienated work I do for my employer because I need to earn a living and the non-alienated work I freely choose to do for myself or because I believe in it, which includes writing for *International Socialism* and selling *Socialist Worker* and would include growing flowers in the garden if I did it. Of all the characteristics of alienated labour identified by Marx the most fundamental is that 'for the worker...it is not his own work but for someone else, that in work he does not belong to himself but to another person'. This is true of the labour of the car mechanic who works for Kwikfit. It is not true of the labour that same mechanic expends on fixing her car on Sunday morning.

Chris fails to grasp this distinction because of two confusions. First he confuses art and artists being affected by alienation, alienated labour and capitalism in general with whether or not their art is the product of alienated labour. Second he confuses the commodification of art works with the alienation of artistic labour. Of course artists as people are *affected* by alienation and so is their art. Alienation is rooted in the relationship of the immediate producers to their work but from this root it pervades and affects every aspect of society—religion, philosophy, sex, sport and naturally, art—and I have never suggested otherwise.[6] Indeed many artists are palpably deeply alienated individuals (Van Gogh, Pollock, Kafka for example) and art, especially modern art, frequently tackles alienation as a theme and not infrequently succumbs to its pressures. This was, and frankly I would have expected Chris to notice this, a central argument in my review of the Royal Academy 'Sensation' exhibition in *International Socialism* 79. However, it is *not* the same as the artist having lost possession or control of their labour.

In several passages Chris seems to equate commodification of the art work with the alienation of artistic labour:

(a) 'But with the spread of commodity production into every nook and cranny of social life, a straightforward distinction between commercial and artistic production becomes extremely difficult'.[7]

(b) '...the undeniably commercial and therefore alienated fields of film, architecture or popular music'.[8]

(c) 'The activity of the artist attempts a self-expression that is denied in alienated labour. But once artists are at the mercy of the market alienation is reintroduced... Once their work is produced even partially in response to external necessities the artist is no longer in control of their own creativity'.[9]

There is very little precision in the writing here. Passage (a) says a straightforward distinction' is 'extremely difficult'. Does that mean a subtle distinction is possible? Passage (b) speaks of the 'undeniably commercial' fields of film, architecture and popular music. Are the fields of theatre, art dealing and classical music less commercialised? What does passage (c) mean by the reintroduction of alienation—when and how did it go away? And why does a relative in the first half of the last sentence ('even *partially* in response') turn into an absolute in the second half ('no longer in control of their creativity')? Nevertheless it is clear that if commodification of product does equal alienation of labour then Chris needs no other argument to refute my position since it is an undeniable empirical fact, and one I acknowledged in my article,[10] that capitalism brings about the commodification of works of art, in all fields of art. But commodification of the product does not equal commodification of the labour that produces the product, nor does it equal the alienation of that labour. Marx made this clear in a passage I cited in my article:

> *Milton produced* **Paradise Lost** *for the same reason that silkworms produce silk. It was an activity of his nature* [ie unalienated labour—JM]. *Later he sold the product for £5.*[11]

In his first paragraph Chris approvingly quotes Trotsky to the effect that art 'by its very essence' cannot tolerate orders. If he had thought about the meaning of this quote he would have seen that it supports my position but contradicts his. If commodification, by itself, shapes and determines the labour that produces the commodity then, if Trotsky is right, art would have been destroyed since art works have clearly been commodified. Certainly capitalist commodification *threatens* to reach back and completely determine the content and nature of the artistic labour thus negating its character as art, which is why art is always embattled under capitalism,[12] but it does not necessarily succeed. Remember, the majority of artists (and novelists, song writers, poets, film makers etc) accept or actively seek the commodification of their output (they try to sell it) but they also defend their control over the process of production. To give one telling example: Ken Loach had to accept *Land and Freedom* becoming a commodity or the film could not have been made, but if he ceded basic control of the filming to the studio or business sponsors there would have been no point in making it.[13]

Moving on to what Chris sees as the dangers of my position I want first to consider the charge that 'it could easily encourage an uncritical attitude to art'.[14] Now it is true that my definition of art is rooted in and encourages a fundamental bias in favour of art (in all its forms). I believe that, in general, the production and consumption of art is of benefit to human beings, contributing to their spiritual growth and their understanding of the world. This is a bias, or rather a judgement, that is clearly shared by Marx and by all the great classical Marxists. In this respect my attitude to art is analogous to my/our attitude to education and medicine. I defend them despite the fact that the art world, like the education system and the health service, is dominated by the bourgeoisie and distorted by capitalism and despite the fact that some would be artists, like some would be teachers and doctors, do more harm than good. But does my definition lead to an uncritical attitude in the sense of an unwillingness or inability to make the necessary distinctions between good and bad art, the outstanding and the mediocre? I don't think it does and I don't see why it should. In my article on 'Sensation' I attacked Marcus Harvey and the Chapmans and praised (some of) Hirst and Whiteread. In my review of Pollock (*Socialist Review*, April 1999) I say some of his paintings are failures and others are masterpieces. Obviously Chris may disagree with my critical judgements but I don't see how he can deny that I make them.

Chris says—and I think it is intended critically—that for me 'art is fundamentally counterposed to capitalism'.[15] If by this Chris means that I think all or most art is consciously anti-capitalist or that art is bound to move in an anti-capitalist direction or that I underestimate the capacity of the bourgeoisie to co-opt art and use it for its purposes, then he is very wide of the mark. The only senses in which I counterpose art to capitalism are the sense in which Marx wrote 'capitalist production is hostile to...art and poetry' (a quote discussed in my original article) and the sense in which Trotsky wrote:

> *Generally speaking art is an expression of man's need for a harmonious and complete life, that is to say, his need for those major benefits of which a society of classes has deprived him. This is why a protest against reality, either conscious or unconscious, active or passive, optimistic or pessimistic, always forms part of a really creative piece of work.*[16]

Chris also seems to think I underestimated the damage done to art by class society:

> *Isn't the fact that art exists in this 'privileged sphere', separated from the life and concerns of the vast majority, going to have some fairly devastating effects on the art itself? And doesn't this have implications for our attitude to art?*[17]

Obviously the answers to these rhetorical questions are 'yes' and 'yes', and the implications are that we seek to defend art from those devastating effects as far as possible, while encouraging democratic access to art and the development of critical and revolutionary art and at the same time fighting for the overthrow of class society so that, amongst many other things, we conquer the realm of art for the oppressed and liberate art from the constraints under which it has hitherto laboured. But if Chris is implying that in rotten and exploitative societies you only get rotten art or you don't get wonderful art he is palpably wrong, whether we are talking about the slave societies of Ancient Egypt and Greece or the feudal societies of Europe and Asia (check out Trotsky on Dante) or even the horrific capitalism of the 20th century. The interesting question, in my opinion, is why, despite the oppressive nature of society, despite the barbarism that is history, there still exists such magnificent art? The answer, I suspect, has something to do with the nature of human creativity and how it finds expression in unalienated labour.

Few debates on cultural questions last long before the bogey of 'elitism' is raised and, sure enough, Chris cannot resist throwing this charge into the pot. But what does 'elitism' mean in this context? Logically it should mean defending the privileges of the ruling elite, or maintaining that the mass of 'ordinary' people are congenitally inferior, ignorant or incapable of ruling or appreciating art whatsoever. But I doubt that even in the heat of polemic Chris would accuse me of these sins. In fact he makes two specific charges. The first is that my definition of art 'runs the risk of favouring in advance the work of the individual fine artist in their garret who appears to control their productive activity over the collective work of musicians, technicians, actors and so on who produce in the undeniably commercial and therefore alienated fields of film, architecture or popular music'.[18] Well, doubtless I do run this risk, much as if I ride a bicycle I run the risk of falling off, but actually it makes no difference whether the artist is in a garret or an airy studio or whether they work individually or collectively. I suspect Chris is just trying to mobilise stereotypes here. With equal logic he could have claimed that my position 'runs the risk' of favouring the 'free' spontaneity of jazz over the discipline and tradition of the classical symphony, or favouring the individual singer-songwriter Bob Dylan over the collective bourgeois aristocratic corps de ballet.[19]

Chris's second charge is that 'it could even lead us to accept the simplistic and elitist distinctions between "high" and "low" culture so beloved of the right'.[20] Since I did not address this question and Chris offers neither evidence nor argument for his assertion, and since the issue is complex and space is short, I will make only brief comments. First, I do, in general, consider the 'canon' of so called 'high' culture (Shakespeare, Mozart, Picasso etc) superior in quality to most of what is most successful in terms of popularity (*Coronation Street*, Michael Jackson, *Titanic* etc) and I wouldn't mind betting Chris does too. But this does not mean I reject all forms of 'popular' culture or the possibility of outstanding work emerging from these genres (eg Billie Holiday, Charlie Chaplin). Second, Chris himself makes a statement I essentially agree with and think important:

In an important sense the capitalist market [I would say 'system'; it is the same under state capitalism—JM] *also denies artists an audience. By robbing the mass of the population of control over their own labour and therefore over production generally the market robs us—the potential audience—of much of our artistic or aesthetic capacities.*[21]

But these are sentiments that would instantly be condemned as elitist by the kind of anti-intellectual populism (and postmodernism) that is just as beloved of the right as 'high culture' snobbery.

Last but not least comes Chris's claim that my position 'tends to take art out of historical development' and that I imply 'a trajectory for artistic development separate from the rest of society'.[22] I must confess to being temporarily nonplussed here. The idea of art existing outside of history or separate from the rest of society is to me so absurd, so alien, that I was somewhat taken aback and it took me a while to figure out what he meant. Where we really differ—I think—is that I believe it is possible, at least to some extent, for powerful art to develop not outside of history or society but in dialectical opposition to the dominant trajectory of society. This is because, as we all know, historical development is the resultant of opposed forces and there is always resistance, both progressive and reactionary, to the main trajectory. Thus in a society where the main trend is the victory of fascism there can arise a powerful anti-fascist art (Heartfield, Brecht, Picasso's *Guernica* etc). In a feudal society in decline there can be significant art that laments or fears that decline and also significant art that is linked to the rising bourgeoisie. (Shakespeare somehow managed to do all of this.) And in capitalist society in crisis there can be great art that responds to this crisis from a variety of points of view. Chris seems not to believe this or not to understand it. This is the only sense I can make of his claims here and his comment that my expectation of 'late 20th and early 21st century masterpieces' is unsatisfactory.

This brings to a close my direct rebuttal of Chris's case. I want to conclude by reasserting what I see as the advantages of understanding art as the product of unalienated labour. Firstly, it offers a distinctively Marxist criterion for distinguishing between art and non-art but one which is inclusive and non-sectarian—it excludes no significant art form (film, poetry, photography, drama etc.) nor any tendency in art on the grounds of its form, technique or ideology. Secondly, it rejects both the position—which really is elitist—that art is what is produced by artists who are defined by special qualities, innate or acquired, which set them apart from other people and the idealist position that art is just what people say it is. Thirdly, it locates within a Marxist analysis of the fundamental characteristic of the human species, creative social labour and in so doing lays the foundation for (though is not in itself a substitute for) an historical materialist account of the gradual emergence of 'art' as a distinct area of human activity as well as anticipating the eventual reintegration of art within productive labour as a whole in the communist society of the future. Fourthly, it helps us to understand the ongoing complex and contradictory relationship between art and capitalism which combines—on both sides—hostility and dependence, ridicule and adulation, rejection and incorporation and why the great Marxists in the classical tradition have always maintained a critical defence of art and a supportive engagement with it.

Notes

1   C Nineham, 'Art and Alienation: A Reply to John Molyneux', *International Socialism* 82, p75.

2   Ibid, p75.

3   In the instance of Brancusi there was actually a court case held to decide whether or not one of his sculptures was art when it was imported and customs claimed it was scrap metal, not art, and as such liable for scrap metal duty.

4   K Marx, *Early Writings* (London, 1963), pp124-125.

5   C Nineham, op cit, p80.

6   I have to confess to being not a little irritated by the way Chris on several occasions implies or suggests that I regard art, or that my definition of art leads to a view of art, as existing in some kind of 'alienation free zone' or as somehow 'immune' to alienation. Chris writes, 'It seems rash to suggest that artistic production is in a simple way immune from such powerful processes' and '...we are deluding ourselves if we believe that any aspect of our lives completely escapes the alienation imposed by capitalist relations'. It is not just that I did not write this, it is that I wrote the direct opposite:

    By non-alienation labour I do not mean labour that exists 'outside' of capitalism (which is increasingly non-existent), or labour that does not produce commodities (the massive commodification of art under capitalism is obvious)... Still less do I mean that 'artists' are not alienated or that their work does not reflect and express alienation—alienation affects everyone in capitalist society. What I mean is labour that remains under the control and direction of the producer.

    Two points here: first I think it is reasonable to expect Chris to pay closer attention to the argument he is criticising and not to caricature it like this; second if he wishes to deny the existence under capitalism of 'labour under the control and direction of the producer' then how does he account for working class revolutionary activity, for the building of the street barricades or the writing of the *Communist Manifesto* or for resistance and self emancipation as a whole?

7   C Nineham, op cit, p76.

8   Ibid, p77.

9   Ibid, p78.

10   Again it seems to have escaped Chris's attention that in discussing the causes of the crisis of legitimacy of modern art I assign considerable importance to the role of commodification of visual art in the form of extremely expensive luxury items for the super-rich.

11   K Marx, *Theories of Surplus Value*, cited in M Solomon (ed), *Marxism and Art* (Brighton, 1979), p75.

12   And why, as I have already argued, Marx describes 'capitalist production as hostile to...art and poetry'.

13   Underlying Chris's confusions about art and alienation is a deeper misunderstanding of Marx's original theory of alienation itself. Unravelling this misunderstanding takes some time and trouble but is worth it if it leads to greater clarity about this important aspect of Marxism. Chris writes:

> *For Marxists, the root of alienation lies in capitalist exploitation, in the fact that the capitalist owns the means of production in society and runs production for profit. Labour becomes a means to create maximum profit by maximising output. In the process the worker loses control over the finished product and the nature of the product itself is determined by the dictates of the market.*

This formulation makes alienated labour appear as a *consequence*, an *effect* of capitalist exploitation and capitalist relations of production, whereas for Marx alienated labour is *constitutive* of capitalist exploitation and analytically prior to it:

> *The relation of the worker to labour produces the relation of the capitalist to labour... Private property is this product, result, and necessary consequence of externalised labour, of the external relation of the worker to nature and to himself.*
>
> *Private property thus is derived, through analysis, from the concept of externalised labour... But the analysis of this idea shows that though private property appears to be the ground and cause of externalised labour, it is rather a consequence of externalised labour... Wages are a direct result of alienated labour, and alienated labour is the direct cause of private property... As we have found the concept of private property through analysis from the concept of alienated, externalised labour, so we can develop all the categories of political economy with the aid of these two factors, and we shall again find in each category—for example, barter, competition, capital, money—only a particular and developed expression of these primary foundations. (K Marx, 1844 Manuscripts, cited in L D Easton and K H Guddat (ed), Writings of the Young Marx on Philosophy and Society (New York, 1967), pp297-299.)*

Both alienated and unalienated labour existed in pre-capitalist modes of production (as did exploitation, oppression, classes, money, and commodities). Under feudalism, for example, the peasant performs alienated labour when working unpaid on the lord's land but unalienated labour when working to produce his/her own subsistence. (Some of what the peasant produces is sent to market, ie commodified, but that is not the same as the peasant's labour being commodified— or alienated). Capitalism does not invent alienated labour but its development enormously increases and intensifies it precisely because capitalism rests on the commodification of labour power. However, this intensification of alienated labour, and therefore alienation in general, does not totally eliminate all forms of non-alienated labour—including that form which is art which develops in dependence upon but also dialectical opposition to the bulk of alienated labour.

14   C Nineham, op cit, p80.
15   Ibid, p75.
16   L Trotsky, *On Literature and Art* (New York, 1977), p104.
17   C Nineham, op cit, p76.
18   Ibid, p76-77.
19   To this I plead guilty, but I also think Chris fails to practise what he preaches here. When he writes about Courbet and Cézanne, artists he rightly admires, he somehow fails to mention the canvas manufacturers, paintbrush makers, models etc whose collective labour contributed to their paintings. And when he discusses *Battleship Potemkin* or *The Threepenny Opera* does he remember to credit the actors and technicians or does he, like the rest of us, just say Eisenstein and Brecht? And does this make him an elitist or is it that he recognises that it is the labour of Courbet and Cézanne, Eisenstein and Brecht that is of principal significance in determining the works' artistic character.
20   C Nineham, op cit, p80.
21   Ibid, p78.
22   Ibid, p81.

Dreams of equality: the levelling poor of the English Revolution

A review of Brian Manning, **The Far Left in the English Revolution 1640 to 1660** *(Bookmarks, 1999), £7.95*

JUDY COX

A historian once described the history of the 17th century as 'a battle-ground which has been heavily fought over...beset with mines, booby-traps and ambushes manned by ferocious scholars prepared to fight every inch of the way'. Standard histories traditionally interpreted the events of the 1640s as a civil war between different wings of the ruling class. However, the Marxist interpretation, pioneered by Christopher Hill, centred on the conflict between two classes, the old aristocracy and the emerging bourgeoisie, with the bourgeoisie being propelled to greater militancy by the poorer sections of society. According to this account, the revolution shifted the balance of power decisively in favour of the emerging capitalists, and in turn facilitated the Industrial Revolution of the 18th century.

Yet despite the ongoing controversy which surrounds interpretations of the revolution, one important element has been neglected by historians: while many have examined the role of the aristocracy and the 'middling sort' in the events of the mid-17th century, few have given equal weight to the role played by the poor. Brian Manning's new book makes an important contribution to the Marxist interpretation of the English Revolution, and also redresses this imbalance by focusing on the role of the poor and those who spoke for them. In order to do this, Manning seeks out the far left of the revolutionary movement, those who stood to the left of the leaderships of the radical Levellers, Fifth Monarchists and Quakers. The English Revolution was a bourgeois revolution, not a socialist revolution. However, as Engels pointed out in his *Socialism, Utopian and Scientific*, 'In every great bourgeois movement there were independent outbursts of that class which was the more or less developed forerunner of the modern proletariat', and at the heart of Manning's book is his brilliant account of the groups that based themselves on those forerunners.

One of the great strengths of this book, besides the wealth of historical detail which Manning brings to the subject, is the weight he gives to the writings of the revolutionary tradition. This aspect of the book ensures it will find an audience amongst many who are not already familiar with the history of the English Revolution. Manning's investigation of the far left wing is interwoven with insights into the process of revolution itself drawn from Marx, Engels, Trotsky, Lenin, Gramsci and Lukács. Thus this book achieves much more than its stated aim: it illuminates the previously shadowy figures of the poor in the revolution and at the same time applies a Marxist analysis of historical change and the revolutionary process to a particular historical situation.

Royalists, parliamentarians and soldiers

Placing the English Revolution firmly in the tradition of great revolutionary upheavals, Manning turns to Trotsky's theory of dual power to explain how the class conflict at the heart of the revolution developed, how two classes competing for power could coexist, albeit uneasily, for a limited time: 'The English Revolution of the 17th century...affords a clear example of the alternating dual power, with sharp transitions in the form of civil war.' Manning develops this further, pointing out that the old order collapsed in 1642 but for the next three years neither the royalists nor the parliamentarians won a decisive victory. The crucial parliamentarian victory at the Battle of Naseby in 1645 ushered in an era of further conflict between the moderate parliamentarians and the highly political New Model Army led by Oliver Cromwell. Ultimately, state power hung between two distinct classes—the old order (the monarchy, the House of the Lords, and the church) and an aspiring class (the House of Commons, the merchants of the City of London, and army officers). Cromwell seized power because neither class seemed capable of imposing itself decisively on the situation.[1]

The conflict between the king and his court, and the wealthy merchants and landowners represented in parliament, has traditionally been used to reinforce the idea that the 1640s was merely a political revolution made by one faction of the ruling class against another. However, Manning argues that the divisions at the top of society should not disguise the role played by those at the bottom of the social hierarchy.

During the revolution it was the poor who formed the backbone of the parliamentary forces and, in 1649, it was the poor, those who had no interest in maintaining the hierarchy and economic inequality of society, who were the basis for any extension of the revolution.

The middling sort and the poor

'The poor' were not one homogenous group. Using the premise which Marx outlined in *The Communist Manifesto*, that the whole history of mankind has been a history of class struggle, Manning explains how that struggle was being transformed in the 17th century. The majority of the poor combined working the land, either their own small plot or common land, with selling any surplus on the market: they were small or petty producers. However, as capitalist methods of production developed through the extension of the market, increasing numbers of the rural poor found their access to land denied. Many were separated from the means of producing what they needed to live, and thus had to sell their labour power for wages. As Marx wrote, 'The expropriation of the great mass of the people from the soil, from the means of subsistence, and from the means of labour, this fearful and painful expropriation of the mass of the people forms the prelude to the history of capital.'

This process was just beginning to have an impact on society in the mid-17th century, so it was the small producers who were the driving force of the English Revolution. Manning gives a fascinating account of the concerns of this class of people. Many groups articulated the resentment of the poor against the rich, but the Levellers and others also defended private property in order to safeguard the small producers' ownership of the means of production. This class of small producers was capable of being extremely radical in defence of its own interests but, Manning argues, it is uncertain whether it was capable of developing a consistent revolutionary consciousness and organisation, as it was both exploited and the exploiter of family, servants, and so on: 'The germs both of proletarian and industrial capitalist class consciousness were already contained in the craftsmen'.[2] The revolution helped to crystallise these emerging forces: the richer farmers became agrarian capitalists who supported the enclosures of the land which so devastated the lives of their poorer neighbours. Other, less fortunate, artisans and farmers were forced to join the ranks of the wage labourers.

The concerns of the labouring poor, as opposed to the farmers and artisans, were articulated by the most radical groups, such as the Diggers. Gerrard Winstanley, the Digger leader, wrote how wage labourers had their labour stolen from them and campaigned for the abolition of wage labour. Their alternative was the communal cultivation of the land, which was to be held in common ownership. The Diggers' movement was crushed by the landowners, but Manning argues that their political ideas indicated that full time wage workers did develop the potential to form their own distinct class consciousness, a consciousness which shaped the egalitarian ideas put forward by the far left in the revolution.

Although the small producers and the labouring poor were often indistinguishable from each other in social status and political aims, Manning gives fascinating and suggestive descriptions of what was beginning to divide them as the labouring poor took their first tentative steps towards becoming a class in their own right. Manning provides a brilliant political context for the development of the poor as a political force, explaining how their ideas and their actions reinforced each other. He quotes Trotsky: 'The immediate causes of the events of a revolution are changes in the state of mind of the conflicting classes. Changes in the collective consciousness have naturally a semi-concealed character. Only when they have attained a certain degree of intensity do the new moods and ideas break to the surface'. Manning combines this with Engels' description of how revolutionary struggles work on the minds of the participants and onlookers until they explode in new political and religious ideas but remain within the assumptions created by the economic conditions of the different social groups.

The godly poor and the levelling poor

This understanding of how revolutionary ideas can remain embedded in assumptions inherited from past provides the basis for looking beneath the religious language which can disguise revolutionary intentions of 17th century radicals. Manning's account of the contradictory role of religion in the 17th century sheds light on the ideology of that age and on the power of some religions today. Royalists, parliamentarians and the far left all claimed biblical justifications for their actions: '...the culture common to both upper and lower classes was a biblical culture, which could be interpreted in two ways—to defend the existing order or to attack the existing order. It contained within it subversive possibilities when transmitted through the experiences and traditions of the poor, and presented the potential for carrying the revolution to more extreme social changes'.[3] For the far left in the English Revolution, religion expressed class conflict and the overwhelming desire for economic equality. As Manning explains, 'Invoking religious sanction for equality was revolutionary because it allowed for the overthrow of the existing economic and social order and its replacement by a wholly different one based on Christian equality'.[4]

Manning gives a real flavour of the heated biblical disputes which were conducted in taverns and markets as ordinary people began get to involved in the revolution. These religious debates often concerned competing political strategies. The far left developed their own brand of 'practical Christianity' which drew its strength not from theology and sermons but from actively helping those in need. This practical Christianity went beyond charity to call for the redistribution of wealth, 'to empty the fullest bags, and pluck down the highest plumes'.[5] The god they appealed to was a levelling god, a god of class revenge, described here by Digger leader Abiezer Coppe: 'For lo I come (says the Lord) with a vengeance, to level also…your honour, pomp, greatness, superfluity, and confound it into parity, equality, community; that the neck of horrid pride, murder, malice, and tyranny, etc may be chopped off at one blow.'

Manning's book reveals how the far left of the English Revolution can be seen as providing the fertile seed bed from which socialist ideas would grow. The low level of social development in the 17th century limited the scope of the radicals, both in terms of the strength of the social groups they represented and of their ideas. Many believed divine intervention would achieve their revolution and that god would level society for them, but the experience of revolution did pull in the opposite direction. In a wonderful quote from Gerrard Winstanley, Manning reveals how the radicals understood the disarming role religion could play: 'For while men are gazing up at heaven, imaging after a happiness, or fearing a hell after they are dead, their eyes are put out, and they see not what is their birthright, and what is to be done by them here on earth while they are living'.[6] Armed with such views, many decided to give their levelling god a helping hand.

The Diggers went furthest in carrying out the will of god through their own actions. 'The Digger colony on St George's Hill was intended to be the first stage in a sort of general strike against wage labour'.[7] Such strikes would have required a far greater level of organisation than that of which the small bands of Diggers were capable, and the strikes which took place during the revolution were hard to sustain as wage labourers were isolated and under the scrutiny of their employers. The emerging proletariat was, in the words of Eduard Bernstein, as yet 'an inchoate class'. But in many ways the strategies they attempted and the goals they fought for have a surprisingly familiar ring to socialists today.

Manning draws a distinction usually applied to the Chartist movement, between 'moral force' radicalism of groups like the Diggers who relied on persuasion and symbolic actions, and 'physical force' radicalism which sought to overthrow the regime through armed uprisings. However, he points out that the two wings were not mutually exclusive: manifestos and peaceful demonstrations were seen as compatible with armed revolt and many radicals combined the two strategies. Manning examines two revolts in order to illustrate this point. The stories of these revolts make exciting reading but the narratives also indicate how the course of the revolution was not predetermined or inevitable but was punctuated by attempts to force it into more radical channels.

Revolt in the army

The first uprising Manning looks at is the Corporal's Revolt of 1649. Corporal William Thompson was dismissed from the army for brawling, became close to the Leveller John Lilburne and agitated among the soldiers. He was court-marshalled for attempting to stir up mutinies in solidarity with the Leveller army revolt of 1647 but he escaped his death sentence. After the regimental revolts which ended at Burford in May 1649, Thompson and around 120 comrades launched an insurrection at Banbury. Thompson went beyond inciting soldiers to mutiny and called for a rebellion against cruelty, tyranny and oppression. After being routed by troops loyal to the republic, Thompson and about 12 companions were isolated and eventually overrun by army regiments. Thompson was killed in this encounter.

This uprising receives little attention today, but contemporaries considered it to be more threatening than the Diggers' commune: Thompson was called the General of the Levellers, and Thompson the Great. Neither was Thompson an isolated, congenitally violent fanatic, as some historians have argued. He enacted a physical force Levellerism which was not an aberration. For example, John Lilburne called for armed revolt when he and others were arrested in March 1649. At this point armed insurrection was an option being considered by many beyond the ranks of Thompson and his band of insurrectionaries. They were being propelled in that direction by events, by the establishment of an army dictatorship and the use of force against the Levellers themselves. There was also a continuity between Thompson's insurrection and the political strategy of the Diggers. As Manning explains:

> *William Thompson and Gerrard Winstanley were both revolutionaries. Thompson sought primarily a political revolution and Winstanley primarily a social revolution, and Thompson pursued his objective by physical force and Winstanley by moral force. However, revolution truly is directed at both social and political transformation and involves continuity between moral and physical force.*[8]

Revolt in the church

Thompson's revolt was based on one of the two great centres of radicalism in the revolution, the army. The Coopers' Revolt in 1657 was based on the other, the congregations of the dissident religious sects. Thomas Venner was the leader of a Fifth Monarchist congregation in Swann Alley, London. The congregation was made up of small producers and artisans. They believed that the kingdom of Jesus Christ was coming but thought they could hasten his arrival: 'Their millennial dreams were sharpened by poverty and they had no social position at stake to restrain them.' Venner and his congregation published a declaration inviting the people to stand up for Christ and their own liberties, and called for revolt to replace King Oliver with King Jesus. They called for a raft of reforms, indicating that they hoped to inspire a mass movement. Large numbers of copies of their programme were printed and distributed around London by the sisters of the congregation. Their planned revolt was nipped in the bud by a troop of horse sent by the government to arrest the revolutionaries. They were caught as they prayed for the success of their revolt in a house in Shoreditch, surrounded by weapons and military provisions. While the number committed to the rebellion was small (between 40 and 300), they expected thousands to flock to their standard. Venner and his comrades were imprisoned until just before the Restoration in 1660 but in January 1661 the irrepressible Venner launched another revolt on the city of London. It was soon crushed, but not until the city was thrown into panic, as documented by diarist Samuel Pepys.

The seedbeds of socialism

The outbursts of independent activity by the poor which Engels described remained isolated and were often strangled at birth, or in early infancy, because the classes they represented were not yet coherent enough to sustain independent organisation. But they were significant. They showed the possibilities which the revolution opened up, and began the discussions which have continued to be central to the working class movement. The debates which engaged the English revolutionaries—whether to wait for divine intervention from above or take direct action, whether to rely on moral force or physical force (or a combination of the two), how to stir the masses into action—were debates which rose again in the Chartist movement of the 19th century, and in every mass movement since. The 17th century radicals dreamt of a society of equality and freedom, the same dream which inspired the the Utopian Socialists two centuries later. The experience of the Chartists and the writings of the Utopian Socialists were drawn on by Marx and Engels as they formulated the theory which could show how to make the Diggers' dream of equality a real possibility.

The Far Left in the English Revolution is a brilliant book. It gives an exciting flavour of the revolutionary possibilities in our past, without sacrificing its theoretical clarity. It deepens our understanding of the forces whose struggles shaped the outcome of the English Revolution and it encourages a deeper understanding of a Marxist account of historical change and what makes a revolution. Manning's account of the revolution helps to illuminate aspects of the revolution such as the shifts in consciousness, the changing relationship between ideology and experience, and the question of state power. All of this means it is a book which helps us understand the past as part of the future.

Notes

1   It was also the largest concentration of wage labourers in the country, and sharp class divisions existed in the army. In the 1640s the rank and file demonstrated deep political consciousness, which turned to disillusionment in the 1650s under Cromwell's Protectorate. By 1659 soldiers were owed £900,000, and when Charles II promised to pay all arrears, the soldiers proved just as decisive in the restoration of the monarchy as they had in its overthrow.

2   K Kautsky, quoted in B Manning, *The Far Left in the English Revolution 1640-1660* (Bookmarks, 1999), p20.

3   Ibid, p34.

4   Ibid, p40.

5   Quoted ibid, p45.

6   Quoted ibid, p77.

7   C Hill, quoted ibid, p64.

8   Ibid, p111.

New books from...

BOOKMARKS PUBLICATIONS

The Balkans, Nationalism and Imperialism

Edited by Lindsey German, price £6.50 (plus £1 p&p)

This book traces the collapse of Yugoslavia, the descent into civil war and ethnic cleansing, and continues up to the most recent disastrous war, in Kosovo. It shows that Western intervention in the Balkans has been disastrous from the very beginning and goes on to explain that NATO bombed Serbia and Kosovo, not on humanitarian grounds, but because of old fashioned imperialism.

The Far Left in the English Revolution 1640 to 1660

Brian Manning, price £7.95 (plus £1.20 p&p)

Brian Manning shows that both in theory and practice the most radical elements in the English Revolution foreshadowed the development of working class consciousness and revolutionary socialist politics.
'This is a book for our time. The struggle for democracy, peace and social justice still goes on and we have much to learn from the English Revolution.'
Tony Benn

Scotland, Class and Nation

Edited by Chris Bambery, price £8.95 (plus £1.35 p&p)

This set of original essays by Angus Calder, Alex Callinicos, Chris Bambery, Neil Davidson and others attempts to revive a discussion and debate about Scottish culture and history in general and working class history in particular.

All available from Bookmarks, 1 Bloomsbury Street, London WC1B 3QE. Phone 0171 637 1848. Fax 0171 637 3416

The Socialist Workers Party is one of an international grouping of socialist organisations:

AUSTRALIA   International Socialists, PO Box A338, Sydney South

BRITAIN   Socialist Workers Party, PO Box 82, London E3

CANADA   International Socialists, PO Box 339, Station E, Toronto, Ontario M6H 4E3

CYPRUS   Ergatiki Demokratia, PO Box 7280, Nicosia

DENMARK   Internationale Socialister, PO Box 5113, 8100 Aarhus C

GERMANY   Linksruck, Postfach 304 183, 20359 Hamburg

GREECE   Sosialistiko Ergatiko Komma, c/o Workers Solidarity, PO Box 8161, Athens 100 10

HOLLAND   Internationale Socialisten, PO Box 92052, 1090AA Amsterdam

IRELAND   Socialist Workers Party, PO Box 1648, Dublin 8

NEW ZEALAND   Socialist Workers Organization, PO Box 8851, Auckland

NORWAY   Internasjonale Socialisterr, Postboks 9226 Grønland, 0134 Oslo

POLAND   Solidarność Socjalistyczna, PO Box 12, 01-900 Warszawa 118

SPAIN   Socialismo Internacional, Apartado 563, 08080 Barcelona

UNITED STATES   International Socialist Organisation, PO Box 16085, Chicago, Illinois 60616

ZIMBABWE   International Socialist Organisation, PO Box 6758, Harare

The following issues of *International Socialism* (second series) are available price £3 (including postage) from IS Journal, PO Box 82, London E3 3LH. *International Socialism* 2:58 and 2:65 are available on cassette from the Royal National Institute for the Blind (Peterborough Library Unit). Phone 01733 370777.

International Socialism 2:83 Summer 1999
John Rees: The socialist revolution and the democratic revolution ★ Mike Haynes: Theses on the Balkan War ★ Angus Calder: Into slavery: the rise of imperialism ★ Jim Wolfreys: The physiology of barbarism ★ John Newsinger: Scenes from the class war: Ken Loach and socialist cinema ★

International Socialism 2:82 Spring 1999
Lindsey German: The Blair project cracks ★ Dan Atkinson and Larry Elliott: Reflating Keynes: a different view of the crisis ★ Peter Morgan: The new Keynesians: staking a hold in the system? ★ Rob Hoveman: Brenner and crisis: a critique ★ Chris Nineham: Art and alienation: a reply to John Molyneux ★ Paul McGarr: Fascists brought to book ★ Brian Manning: Revisionism revised ★ Neil Davidson: In perspective: Tom Nairn ★

International Socialism 2:81 Winter 1998
Alex Callinicos: World capitalism at the abyss ★ Mike Haynes and Pete Glatter: The Russian catastrophe ★ Phil Marfleet: Globalisation and the Third World ★ Lindsey German: In a class of its own ★ Judy Cox: John Reed: reporting on the revolution ★ Kevin Ovenden: The resistible rise of Adolf Hitler ★

International Socialism 2:80 Autumn 1998
Clare Fermont: Indonesia: the inferno of revolution ★ Workers' representatives and socialists: Three interviews from Indonesia ★ Chris Bambery: Report from Indonesia ★ Tony Cliff: Revolution and counter-revolution: lessons for Indonesia ★ John Molyneux: The legitimacy of modern art ★ Gary McFarlane: A respectable trade? Slavery and the rise of capitalism ★ Paul McGarr: The French Revolution: Marxism versus capitalism ★ Shaun Doherty: Will the real James Connolly please stand up? ★

International Socialism 2:79 Summer 1998
John Rees: The return of Marx? ★ Lindsey German: Reflections on *The Communist Manifesto* ★ Judy Cox: An introduction to Marx's theory of alienation ★ Judith Orr: Making a comeback: the Marxist theory of crisis ★ Megan Trudell: New Labour, old conflicts: the story so far ★ John Molyneux: State of the art ★ Anna Chen: In perspective: Sergei Eisenstein ★ Jonathan Neale: Vietnam veterans ★ Phil Gasper: Bookwatch: Marxism and science ★

International Socialism 2:78 Spring 1998
Colin Sparks: The eye of the storm ★ Shin Gyoung-hee: The crisis and the workers' movement in South Korea ★ Rob Hoveman: Financial crises and the real economy ★ Peter Morgan: Class divisions in the gay community ★ Alex Callinicos: The secret of the dialectic ★ John Parrington: It's life, Jim, but not as we know it ★ Judy Cox: Robin Hood: earl, outlaw or rebel? ★ Ian Birchall: The vice-like hold of nationalism? A comment on Megan Trudell's 'Prelude to revolution' ★ William Keach: In perspective: Alexander Cockburn and Christopher Hitchens ★

International Socialism 2:76 Autumn 1997
Mike Haynes: Was there a parliamentary alternative in 1917? ★ Megan Trudell: Prelude to revolution: class consciousness and the First World War ★ Judy Cox: A light in the darkness ★ Pete Glatter: Victor Serge: writing for the future ★ Gill Hubbard: A guide to action ★ Chris Bambery: Review article: Labour's history of hope and despair ★

International Socialism 2:75 Summer 1997
John Rees: The class struggle under New Labour ★ Alex Callinicos: Europe: the mounting crisis ★ Lance Selfa: Mexico after the Zapatista uprising ★ William Keach: Rise like lions? Shelley and the revolutionary left ★ Judy Cox: What state are we really in? ★ John Parrington: In perspective: Valentin Voloshinov ★

International Socialism 2:74 Spring 1997
Colin Sparks: Tories, Labour and the crisis in education ★ Colin Wilson: The politics of information technology ★ Mike Gonzalez: No more heroes: Nicaragua 1996 ★ Christopher Hill: Tulmults and commotions: turning the world upside down ★ Peter Morgan: Capitalism without frontiers? ★ Alex Callinicos: Minds, machines and evolution ★ Anthony Arnove: In perspective: Noam Chomsky★

International Socialism 2:73 Winter 1996
Chris Harman: Globalisation: a critique of a new orthodoxy ★ Chris Bambery: Marxism and sport ★ John Parrington: Computers and consciousness: a reply to Alex Callinicos ★ Joe Faith: Dennett, materialism and empiricism ★ Megan Trudell: Who made the American Revolution? ★ Mark O'Brien: The class conflicts which shaped British history ★ John Newsinger: From class war to Cold War ★ Alex Callinicos: The state in debate ★ Charlie Kimber: Review article: coming to terms with barbarism in Rwanda in Burundi★

International Socialism 2:72 Autumn 1996
Alex Callinicos: Betrayal and discontent: Labour under Blair ★ Sue Cockerill and Colin Sparks: Japan in crisis ★ Richard Levins: When science fails us ★ Ian Birchall: The Babeuf bicentenary: conspiracy or revolutionary party? ★ Brian Manning: A voice for the poor ★ Paul O'Flinn: From the kingdom of necessity to the kingdom of freedom: Morris's *News from Nowhere* ★ Clare Fermont: Bookwatch: Palestine and the Middle East 'peace process'★

International Socialism 2:71 Summer 1996
Chris Harman: The crisis of bourgeois economics ★ Hassan Mahamdallie: William Morris and revolutionary Marxism ★ Alex Callinicos: Darwin, materialism and revolution ★ Chris Nineham: Raymond Williams: revitalising the left? ★ Paul Foot: A passionate prophet of liberation ★ Gill Hubbard: Why has feminism failed women? ★ Lee Sustar: Bookwatch: fighting to unite black and white★

International Socialism 2:70 Spring 1996
Alex Callinicos: South Africa after apartheid ★ Chris Harman: France's hot December ★ Brian Richardson: The making of a revolutionary ★ Gareth Jenkins: Why Lucky Jim turned right—an obituary of Kingsley Amis ★ Mark O'Brien: The bloody birth of capitalism ★ Lee Humber: Studies in revolution ★ Adrian Budd: A new life for Lenin ★ Martin Smith: Bookwatch: the General Strike★

International Socialism 2:69 Winter 1995
Lindsey German: The Balkan war: can there be peace? ★ Duncan Blackie: The left and the Balkan war ★ Nicolai Gentchev: The myth of welfare dependency ★ Judy Cox: Wealth, poverty and class in Britain today ★ Peter Morgan: Trade unions and strikes ★ Julie Waterson: The party at its peak ★ Megan Trudell: Living to some purpose ★ Nick Howard: The rise and fall of socialism in one city ★ Andy Durgan: Bookwatch: Civil war and revolution in Spain ★

International Socialism 2:68 Autumn 1995
Ruth Brown: Racism and immigration in Britain ★ John Molyneux: Is Marxism deterministic? ★ Stuart Hood: News from nowhere? ★ Lee Sustar: Communism in the heart of the beast ★ Peter Linebaugh: To the teeth and forehead of our faults ★ George Paizis: Back to the future ★ Phil Marshall: The children of stalinism ★ Paul D'Amato: Bookwatch: 100 years of cinema ★

International Socialism 2:67 Summer 1995
Paul Foot: When will the Blair bubble burst? ★ Chris Harman: From Bernstein to Blair—100 years of revisionism ★ Chris Bambery: Was the Second World War a war for democracy? ★ Alex Callinicos: Hope against the Holocaust ★Chris Nineham: Is the media all powerful? ★ Peter Morgan: How the West was won ★ Charlie Hore: Bookwatch: China since Mao ★

International Socialism 2:66 Spring 1995
Dave Crouch: The crisis in Russia and the rise of the right ★ Phil Gasper: Cruel and unusual punishment: the politics of crime in the United States ★ Alex Callinicos: Backwards to liberalism ★ John Newsinger: Matewan: film and working class struggle ★ John Rees: The light and the dark ★ Judy Cox: How to make the Tories disappear ★ Charlie Hore: Jazz: a reply to the critics ★ Pat Riordan: Bookwatch: Ireland ★

International Socialism 2:65 Special issue
Lindsey German: Frederick Engels: life of a revolutionary ★ John Rees: Engels' Marxism ★ Chris Harman: Engels and the origins of human society ★ Paul McGarr: Engels and natural science ★

International Socialism 2:63 Summer 1994
Alex Callinicos: Crisis and class struggle in Europe today ★ Duncan Blackie: The United Nations and the politics of imperialism ★ Brian Manning: The English Revolution and the transition from feudalism to capitalism ★ Lee Sustar: The roots of multi-racial labour unity in the United States ★ Peter Linebaugh: Days of villainy: a reply to two critics ★ Dave Sherry: Trotsky's last, greatest struggle ★ Peter Morgan: Geronimo and the end of the Indian wars ★ Dave Beecham: Ignazio Silone and *Fontamara* ★ Chris Bambery: Bookwatch: understanding fascism ★

International Socialism 2:62 Spring 1994
Sharon Smith: Mistaken identity—or can identity politics liberate the oppressed? ★ Iain Ferguson: Containing the crisis—crime and the Tories ★ John Newsinger: Orwell and the Spanish Revolution ★ Chris Harman: Change at the first millenium ★ Adrian Budd: Nation and empire—Labour's foreign policy 1945-51 ★ Gareth Jenkins: Novel questions ★ Judy Cox: Blake's revolution ★ Derek Howl: Bookwatch: the Russian Revolution ★

International Socialism 2:61 Winter 1994
Lindsey German: Before the flood? ★ John Molyneux: The 'politically correct' controversy ★ David McNally: E P Thompson—class struggle and historical materialism ★ Charlie Hore: Jazz—a people's music ★ Donny Gluckstein: Revolution and the challenge of labour ★ Charlie Kimber: Bookwatch: the Labour Party in decline ★

International Socialism 2:59 Summer 1993
Ann Rogers: Back to the workhouse ★ Kevin Corr and Andy Brown: The labour aristocracy and the roots of reformism ★ Brian Manning: God, Hill and Marx ★ Henry Maitles: Cutting the wire: a criticial appraisal of Primo Levi ★ Hazel Croft: Bookwatch: women and work ★

International Socialism 2:58 Spring 1993
Chris Harman: Where is capitalism going? (part one) ★ Ruth Brown and Peter Morgan: Politics and the class struggle today: a roundtable discussion ★ Richard Greeman: The return of Comrade Tulayev: Victor Serge and the tragic vision of Stalinism ★ Norah Carlin: A new English revolution ★ John Charlton: Building a new world ★ Colin Barker: A reply to Dave McNally ★

International Socialism 2:56 Autumn 1992
Chris Harman: The Return of the National Question ★ Dave Treece: Why the Earth Summit failed ★ Mike Gonzalez: Can Castro survive? ★ Lee Humber and John Rees: The good old cause—an interview with Christopher Hill ★ Ernest Mandel: The Impasse of Schematic Dogmatism ★

International Socialism 2:55 Summer 1992
Alex Callinicos: Race and class ★ Lee Sustar: Racism and class struggle in the American Civil War era ★ Lindsey German and Peter Morgan: Prospects for socialists—an interview with Tony Cliff ★ Robert Service: Did Lenin lead to Stalin? ★ Samuel Farber: In defence of democratic revolutionary socialism ★ David Finkel: Defending 'October' or sectarian dogmatism? ★ Robin Blackburn: Reply to John Rees ★ John Rees: Dedicated followers of fashion ★ Colin Barker: In praise of custom ★ Sheila McGregor: Revolutionary witness ★

International Socialism 2:54 Spring 1992
Sharon Smith: Twilight of the American dream ★ Mike Haynes: Class and crisis—the transition in eastern Europe ★ Costas Kossis: A miracle without end? Japanese capitalism and the world economy ★ Alex Callinicos: Capitalism and the state system: A reply to Nigel Harris ★ Steven Rose: Do animals have rights? ★ John Charlton: Crime and class in the 18th century ★ John Rees: Revolution, reform and working class culture ★ Chris Harman: Blood simple ★

International Socialism 2:51 Summer 1991
Chris Harman: The state and capitalism today ★ Alex Callinicos: The end of nationalism? ★ Sharon Smith: Feminists for a strong state? ★ Colin Sparks and Sue Cockerill: Goodbye to the Swedish miracle ★ Simon Phillips: The South African Communist Party and the South African working class ★ John Brown: Class conflict and the crisis of feudalism ★

International Socialism 2:49 Winter 1990
Chris Bambery: The decline of the Western Communist Parties ★ Ernest Mandel: A theory which has not withstood the test of time ★ Chris Harman: Criticism which does not withstand the test of logic ★ Derek Howl: The law of value In the USSR ★ Terry Eagleton: Shakespeare and the class struggle ★ Lionel Sims: Rape and pre-state societies ★ Sheila McGregor: A reply to Lionel Sims ★

International Socialism 2:48 Autumn 1990
Lindsey German: The last days of Thatcher ★ John Rees: The new imperialism ★ Neil Davidson and Donny Gluckstein: Nationalism and the class struggle in Scotland ★ Paul McGarr: Order out of chaos ★

International Socialism 2:46 Winter 1989
Chris Harman: The storm breaks ★ Alex Callinicos: Can South Africa be reformed? ★ John Saville: Britain, the Marshall Plan and the Cold War ★ Sue Clegg: Against the stream ★ John Rees: The rising bourgeoisie ★

International Socialism 2:44 Autumn 1989
Charlie Hore: China: Tiananmen Square and after ★ Sue Clegg: Thatcher and the welfare state ★ John Molyneux: *Animal Farm* revisited ★ David Finkel: After Arias, is the revolution over? ★ John Rose: Jews in Poland ★

International Socialism 2:41 Winter 1988
Polish socialists speak out: Solidarity at the Crossroads ★ Mike Haynes: Nightmares of the market ★ Jack Robertson: Socialists and the unions ★ Andy Strouthous: Are the unions in decline? ★ Richard Bradbury: What is Post-Structuralism? ★ Colin Sparks: George Bernard Shaw ★

International Socialism 2:39 Summer 1988
Chris Harman and Andy Zebrowski: Glasnost, before the storm ★ Chanie Rosenberg: Labour and the fight against fascism ★ Mike Gonzalez: Central America after the Peace Plan ★ Ian Birchall: Raymond Williams ★ Alex Callinicos: Reply to John Rees ★

International Socialism 2:35 Summer 1987
Pete Green: Capitalism and the Thatcher years ★ Alex Callinicos: Imperialism, capitalism and the state today ★ Ian Birchall: Five years of *New Socialist* ★ Callinicos and Wood debate 'Looking for alternatives to reformism' ★ David Widgery replies on 'Beating Time' ★

International Socialism 2:30 Autumn 1985
Gareth Jenkins: Where is the Labour Party heading? ★ David McNally: Debt, inflation and the rate of profit ★ Ian Birchall: The terminal crisis in the British Communist Party ★ replies on Women's oppression and *Marxism Today* ★

International Socialism 2:26 Spring 1985
Pete Green: Contradictions of the American boom ★ Colin Sparks: Labour and imperialism ★ Chris Bambery: Marx and Engels and the unions ★ Sue Cockerill: The municipal road to socialism ★ Norah Carlin: Is the family part of the superstructure? ★ Kieran Allen: James Connolly and the 1916 rebellion ★

International Socialism 2:18 Winter 1983
Donny Gluckstein: Workers' councils in Western Europe ★ Jane Ure Smith: The early Communist press in Britain ★ John Newsinger: The Bolivian Revolution ★ Andy Durgan: Largo Caballero and Spanish socialism ★ M Barker and A Beezer: Scarman and the language of racism ★

International Socialism 2:14 Winter 1981
Chris Harman: The riots of 1981 ★ Dave Beecham: Class struggle under the Tories ★ Tony Cliff: Alexandra Kollontai ★ L James and A Paczuska: Socialism needs feminism ★ reply to Cliff on Zetkin ★ Feminists In the labour movement ★